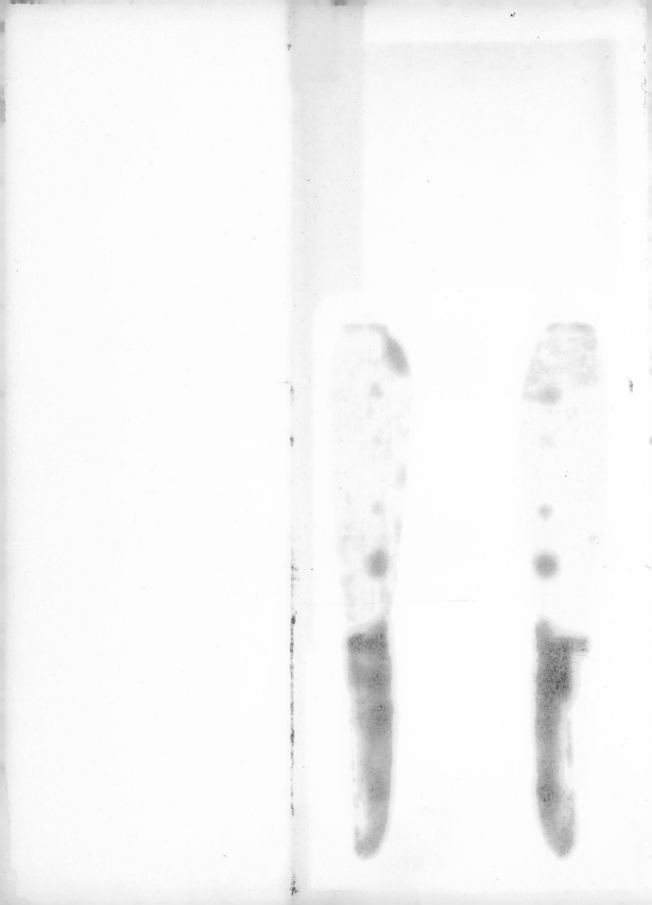

Anne Maile

Author of *Tie-&-Dye as a Present-Day Craft*

TIE-&-DYE MADE EASY

MILLS & BOON LIMITED
London

TAPLINGER PUBLISHING COMPANY
New York

First published 1971 in England by Mills
& Boon Limited, 17-19 Foley Street,
London W1A 1DR and in the United
States by Taplinger Publishing Co., Inc.,
200 Park Avenue, New York N.Y. 10003.

© 1971 Anne Maile
Reprinted 1974

British ISBN 0 263 51710 1

American ISBN 0-8008-7701-2

Library of Congress Catalog
Card Number 72-148406

Printed in Great Britain

Dedicated to my dear husband

Acknowledgements

I should like to thank Mark Gerson FIIP, ARPS, for the Collage colour plates, my nephew Robert Sewell for a few colour plates, and the Editor of *Art and Craft in Education* for allowing reproduction of several photographs.

I am indebted to Dylon International Ltd for their kind co-operation and for generously providing me with dyes.

This is an opportunity to express my admiration and appreciation of the way teachers have successfully introduced tie-and-dye into schools and colleges. They have been a great inspiration to me, and have helped me to reach a realistic estimate of the work that children can do.

At my publishers, I am grateful to Mrs Joan Bryant for her advice and guidance at all times.

Finally I should like to thank my husband for his constant practical help.

AM

Contents

Introduction

Tie-and-dye has now become an established and popular craft. A great many more people wish to find out how to make their own striking and unusual tie-dyed fabrics.

This book contains a large selection of easy ways of creating resist-dyed textures and patterns on cloth. Some require a minimum of skill, enabling the youngest schoolchildren, the handicapped, beginners and all those who want quick results to experiment successfully. The various methods are described in simple language. The step-by-step instructions are fully illustrated with numerous diagrams and photographs.

There are also some new methods and a fresh approach to some of the more traditional techniques which should prove rewarding and stimulating for the experienced tie-dyer.

Suggestions are given to help those teachers who wish to introduce the craft of tie-and-dye to their pupils but have only limited facilities for working or have to exercise the strictest economy in the use of materials. There are ideas for using up odd pieces of tie-and-dye, and several schemes for class projects. Included are photographs of garments, toys, accessories, collages, cut-outs and wall hangings made from tie-dyed fabrics.

Perhaps the most important aspect of this book and the main reason for its existence is to encourage all those people who would like to do tie-and-dye but think it is beyond them. All I can say is "Take the risk! There is great fun in creating and great pleasure in using your own tie-dyed fabrics."

HOW TO DO TIE-&-DYE

The word TIE-AND-DYE describes the two stages of the craft.

First—tie up the cloth.

Second—put the tied-up bundle of cloth in the first dye. Leave it for the required time before taking it out of the dye. Rinse it well in clean water. Put the bundle on some newspaper to drain, and then undo it. It is now a flat piece of cloth again.

If you did the tying up tightly enough, the cloth should have a pattern of dyed and undyed shapes.

The tying-up part is very important. The cloth must be bunched up so closely that the dye cannot reach the inside of the sample. That is why this craft is called "resist-dyeing", because some of the cloth is gripped so tightly it resists the dye. If the bundle is loose the dye soaks right through and the pattern is lost.

Before dyeing your tied-up sample, soak it in clean cold water for a moment. Take it out and squeeze it, or let it drain on newspaper before putting it in the dye. This is called "wetting-out" the sample. This helps to give a much better "resist", because the water inside the bundle keeps out the dye.

For your first experiments use quite small pieces of cotton cloth (old cloth if you have some). Pieces the size of a handkerchief are quite big enough.

To dye a second or third colour:

1. If the sample has been undone after dyeing the first colour, tie it up again. Bring the parts that need more colour to the outside of the bundle.

2. If the sample is still tied up, re-arrange or add more binding.

Wet out if necessary. Dye. Rinse. Drain and untie. When the sample is untied after the final dyeing, rinse again. Drain on newspaper. Iron, covered with clean newspaper, while it is still damp.

WHAT YOU NEED

FABRIC

All kinds of cotton cloth are suitable.
Muslin, lawn, cambric, poplin, calico,*
voile, casement, drill, furnishing cottons,
repp, cotton velvet, velveteen and
corduroy. Scrim. Sheeting—plain, twill
and flannelette. Sateen. Towelling of all
kinds. Cotton satin, organdie. Most types
of linen cloth. Some hessians. Viscose
rayon fabrics. Woollen mixtures such as
Winceyette, Clydella, Viyella and similar
wool and cotton mixtures. Woollen
cloths, flannel, nun's veiling. Woollen
georgette. Silk fabrics, jap silk, silk twill,
wild silk, silk georgette, silk chiffon, panne
velvet, etc.

White or cream fabrics are best, but
pastel colours are quite acceptable.
Avoid fabrics of man-made fibres: these
need special dyes. Crease-resistant and
drip-dry materials do not always take the
dye well. Test a small piece before using.

If possible, wash your cloth before tying
up. This removes any dressing, dirt or
grease, and makes the cloth more
absorbent. If the cloth has *not* been
washed beforehand, tie up the sample,
then do one of the following:

*Unbleached calico is cheap and very
satisfactory. Wash several times in a washing
machine, or boil up with soap powder, or
detergent added. Leave the cloth to soak in
this water until cool—or longer if possible.
Rinse thoroughly.

1. Wash the bundle in hot water with a
little soap powder or detergent added.
Rinse well and squeeze before dyeing.

2. Soak the bundle for a while in hot
water. Rinse in some fresh water.
Squeeze before dyeing.

3. Soak the bundle in cold water for
five minutes. Rinse in some fresh water.
Squeeze before dyeing.

Bondina or Pellon play fabric

This is inexpensive and can be tie-dyed
satisfactorily, but the colours are paler
than when dyed on cotton fabrics. There
are three types of this fabric, fine,
medium and thick. The fine one dyes
better than the other two and the thick
one is the least good. It could be useful
for costumes for school plays, mats,
aprons, book covers, toys, mobiles,
backgrounds for hangings, etc.

The best colour results are from hot
dyeing with household and direct dyes.
Tie up and dye as ordinary cloth.

Very thin fabrics are extremely useful
for dyeing, especially by the folding
methods. When using them for garments,
or parts of garments, they can be
stiffened with all kinds of starch, gum
arabic, iron-on Vilene or Staflex.

DYE VESSELS

Any vessels of enamel, stainless steel and galvanized ware are suitable for hot and cold dyes. Besides these, for *cold* dyes only, any containers which will not rust, made of pot, glass, plastic (but not aluminium) can be used. A washing machine or boiler is ideal for hot or cold bulk dyeing. A plastic dustbin is suitable for bulk cold dyeing. Dyes are dealt with in Chapter 12 on page 130.

THREAD

All kinds of string, twist, bast, yarn, raffia, tape, old nylon stockings. Cotton thread as used by tailors (No 10 and 24), crochet cotton, button-hole thread, ordinary sewing thread and machine cotton (36), all linen threads, especially Nos 18-35, carpet thread, etc. Some threads of man-made fibres are good. Children can collect any pieces of string and thread to use. Have a bag for storing odd pieces of cloth, string and thread, however small, that can be used for tie-dyeing.

NEWSPAPER

Save lots of newspaper. It is useful for all sorts of things.

OTHER EQUIPMENT

Spoons, sticks for stirring the dye

Scissors

Rubber gloves

Overall or apron

Measuring "spoon" scoops

Pins and needles

Pencil, chalk or charcoal

Ruler

Iron

Polythene bags of all sizes

Screw-top jars and bottles

Some metric equivalents

$\frac{1}{4}''$	0.6 cm
$\frac{1}{2}''$	1.25 cm
$\frac{3}{4}''$	1.9 cm
$1''$	2.5 cm
$1\frac{1}{2}''$	3.8 cm
$2''$	5 cm

1
TIE-DYEING
WITH SIMPLE AIDS

No scissors or binding thread will be needed.

Squeeze a piece of cloth in your hands until it is well creased. Then bunch it up tightly into one of the following:

A NET BAG

Any kind will do, nylon, cotton or plastic. The ones that are sold containing nuts and vegetables are very useful. If they have an open mesh use two or three,

one inside the other. When the cloth is bunched up inside the bag, twist it round several times just above the cloth. This helps to tighten it up more. Put a rubber band round the twisted part and over the bundle as well. You can turn the top part of the bag down to go over the bundle again. Put on another rubber band. This will give you a better "resist" when dyeing. Dye the first colour. Undo, and tie up again before dyeing the next colour.

Effect after two dyeings.

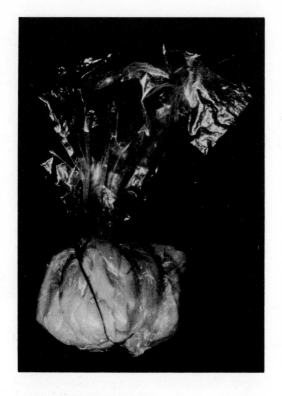

A POLYTHENE BAG

Effect after dyeing.

A small narrow one is best. When the
cloth is bunched inside the bag, twist it
round several times to make a "neck".
Put this bag inside a second polythene
bag. Twist this round above the bundle
of cloth. Put on a rubber band. If the
bag is loose put several rubber bands
round it in all directions. Lastly, prick
through the polythene bags all over with
a pin. This will make small holes so that
the dye can soak through to the cloth.
You can put polythene bags into hot or
cold dyes.

To dye a second colour put the cloth
back again into the polythene bag as
before and add rubber rings.

A small piece after one dyeing.

By this method it is possible to dye pieces of cloth two to three yards in length. This would mean putting some rubber bands at intervals around the tube, to give an even texture.

A. This large sample was dyed dry.
B. This large sample was wetted out before dyeing.

A NYLON STOCKING

Use a single or double stocking. Pack your cloth in quite tightly, because the stocking stretches. Twist the stocking just above the bundle of cloth. Put on a rubber ring. Turn the spare part of the stocking leg down over the bundle again. Twist it and put on a rubber band. The foot part of the stocking can be cut off. If you do this, knot it or put a rubber ring on the cut end before putting in the cloth.

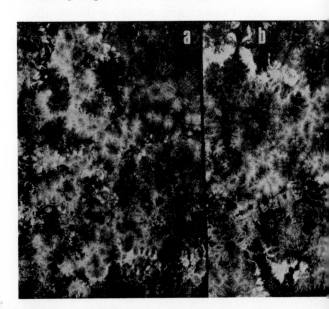

PLASTIC HAIR CURLERS

One curler will only hold a very small piece of cloth. Push your cloth inside the curler and press it down tightly with a pencil or something similar. Put a rubber ring around it to stop the cloth coming out from the top and bottom of the curler. Another way to "stop up" the ends is to put plastic pins, pieces of matchstick or pipe cleaner across the openings or to use corks as plugs.

AN OPEN MESH CLOTH

Look round for old net curtains, nylon shopping bags, household cotton stockinette, etc. Place a single or double piece flat on the table. Screw up the cloth into a ball in your hands. Place it on the net. Gather up all the outside edges of net so that your cloth is completely enclosed. Twist the knob of cloth round several times until it is firm. Put a rubber band just above the knob of cloth, on the "neck" of twisted net. Add some rubber rings or bands around the knob if necessary.

Texture after dyeing.

Result when dyed.

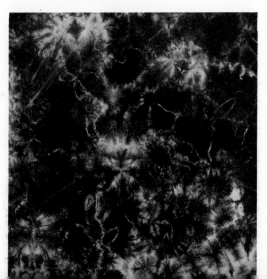

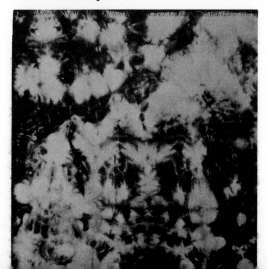

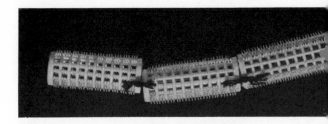

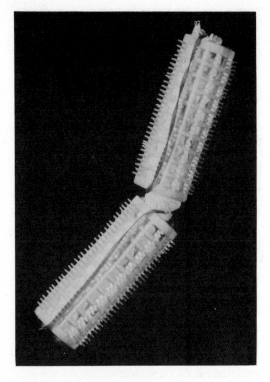

For a longer piece of cloth find a curler which grips the cloth closely when threaded on it like a bead. Form the cloth into a tube and twist it into the first curler. Put a rubber ring round it. Thread the second curler on the other end of the cloth and push this down next to the first curler. Twist the cloth tightly into each curler with a screwing movement. Continue like this until all your cloth is enclosed inside a line of curlers. Several hair curlers can be joined together with string or pipe cleaners to make a long hollow tube to contain the cloth.

Effect after dyeing a larger piece.

A larger piece of cloth in two curlers. Rubber rings keep the cloth in place.

Effect after two dyeings.

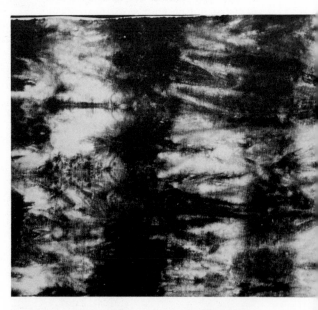

You can leave a gap of cloth about one inch in between each curler. Put a rubber band round it. This gives a stripe effect in the dyed pattern.

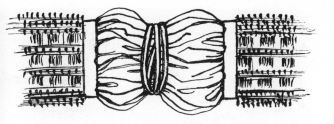

When a curler is too loose, fold your cloth in half across before pushing it in. This makes the cloth bulky enough to fit the curler.

Plastic curlers should not be left too long in very hot dye or they become warped and broken. Cold or warm dyes do not hurt them at all.

When using these "gadget" methods, the pattern may be patchy or uninteresting after dyeing the first colour. Don't worry! Put the cloth back again in its container and dye it a different colour. If you have too much white cloth after the first colour, when dyeing the second colour, use fewer rubber rings and put the sample into the dye DRY.

If you have very little or *no* white cloth left after dyeing the first colour you need to put on more rubber rings to make the bundle much tighter. Also, wet it out before dyeing the second colour.

The ideas above are just a few ways to dye simple textures and patterns. Look around for any similar gadgets that will enclose cloth and will not turn rusty in the dye. Remember, a certain amount of dye must be allowed to penetrate to make the dyed texture. Holes can usually be made with a pin or a nail, if necessary.

PIPE CLEANERS

Small to medium pieces of cloth are best for this method.

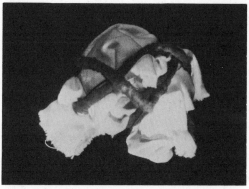

Bunch up your cloth into a ball. Then wrap a pipe cleaner round the bundle. This acts as a binding and forms the resist area, so it must be put on firmly. To fasten off twist the two ends of the pipe cleaner round each other and tuck them under the folds of cloth. Do this carefully because pipe cleaners have rather scratchy ends. Use two or three pipe cleaners if one does not grip the cloth properly.

Marbled pattern after one dyeing.

Twist two pipe cleaners together for one inch to make a longer working length.

Another way to make a strong join is to turn both ends up, hook them together and twist the two small projecting pieces round the main parts of the pipe cleaners.

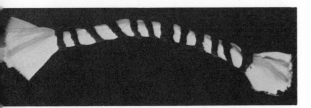

Gather up a small piece of cloth to form a roll. Twist pipe cleaners round it from top to bottom.

Pattern after one dyeing.

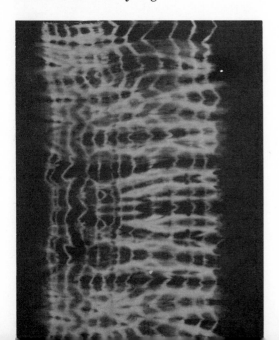

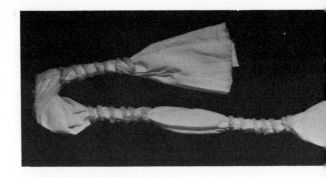

Gather up a longer piece of cloth into a roll. Twist pipe cleaners round it at intervals.

The result is a pattern of stripes.

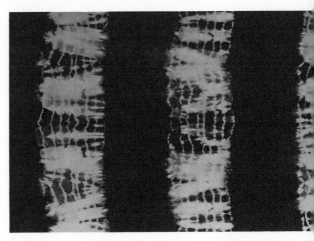

Fold a small square of cloth into quarters. Hold the central point of cloth while twisting one pipe cleaner to form a band just below it.

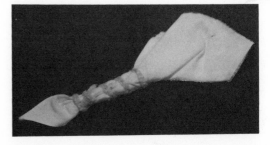

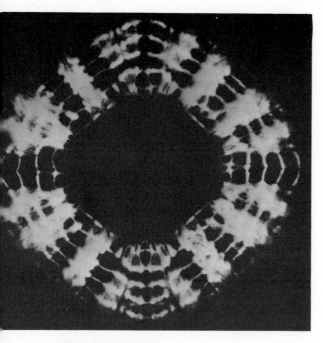

The dyed design.

Fold as previously. Hold the corners opposite the central point and twist on two or three pipe cleaners. Make a more spread-out band of binding.

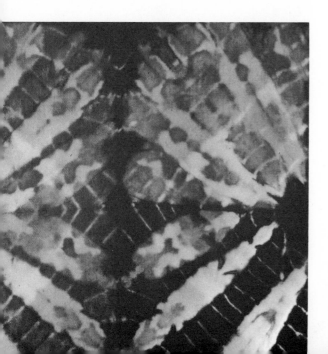

Pipe cleaners can be used over and over again. Straighten them out and dry them. Sometimes the colour from a previous dyeing is transferred to a new sample from the pipe cleaner. Fuse wire can also be used for wrapping round your samples.

CLOTHES PEGS, CLOTHES PINS AND CLIPS

It is surprising how many sophisticated and exciting patterns can be made on small and large pieces of cloth with clothes pegs, clothes pins and clips. Fold or gather up your cloth and just push them on.

Plastic spring pegs or pins are excellent for cold water dyes. They should not be put in very hot dye as this causes them to become distorted and to open: thus the pattern could be spoilt.

Wooden pegs or pins of all kinds are ideal for hot and cold dyes. Wash or rinse after use as they retain the dye. Any pegs or clothes pins containing metal need drying after washing, to prevent them from rusting. After washing, spread them out on a newspaper and place on a radiator, in the oven, or somewhere warm to dry.

Clips of all kinds can be used, so long as they grip the cloth tightly. If you can get stainless steel clips, these are ideal.

Plastic clips unless very sturdy are only suitable for cold dyeing.

Bulldog clips (metal) make really splendid patterns. They are suitable for hot and cold dyeing. Take them off the sample in the final rinse water, or a rust mark might develop. Clips with metal on need drying *immediately*. You can sometimes buy large wooden or plastic clips from shops selling boat equipment.

The pattern effect is quite different, according to whether the peg, clothes pin or clip is put right on the edge of the cloth, or whether it is pushed well over the sample.

To get the best results, using these gadgets, wet out the sample before dyeing. Do not squeeze or they will move. Lift the sample out of the cold water and place on some newspaper to drain. This should be done inside a bowl or on a draining board near a sink. To keep the sample as flat as possible use a wide, shallow dye vessel. Turn the sample over carefully several times during the dyeing process. Rinse well. When the water is clear, take the pegs off the cloth while it is in the water. Unfold the sample and rinse again.

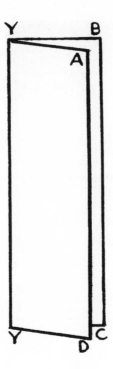

2 Cloth folded in half lengthways.

Methods of folding

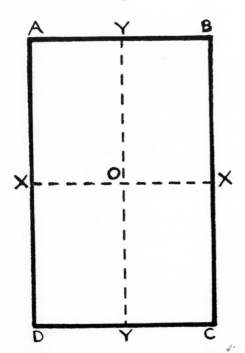

1 Rectangle ABCD, centre point 0. XX and YY the centre points of the four sides.

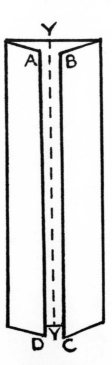

3 Cloth folded in half lengthways where the outside edges meet in the centre.

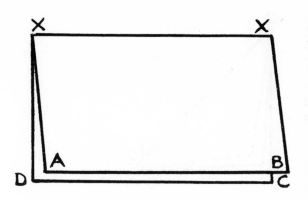

4 Cloth folded in half across.

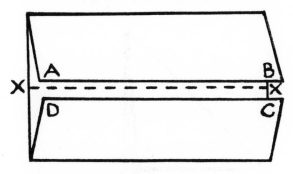

5 Cloth folded in half across with the outside edges meeting in the centre.

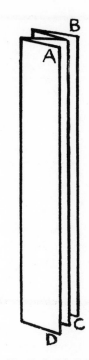

7 Cloth folded in four lengthways.

8 Cloth folded into quarters.

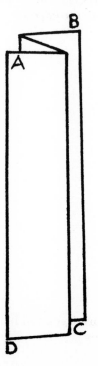

6 Cloth folded in three lengthways.

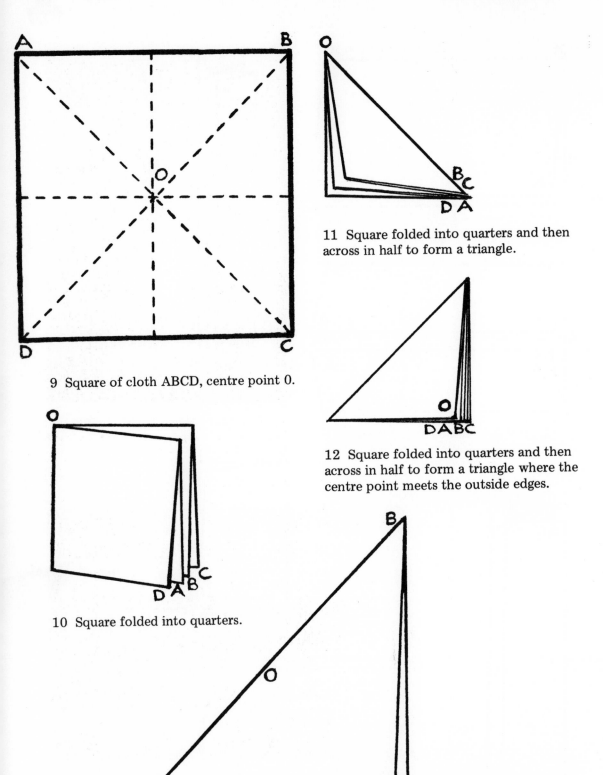

9 Square of cloth ABCD, centre point 0.

10 Square folded into quarters.

11 Square folded into quarters and then across in half to form a triangle.

12 Square folded into quarters and then across in half to form a triangle where the centre point meets the outside edges.

13 Square folded in half diagonally.

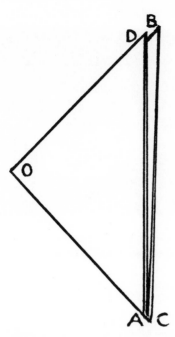

14 A square of cloth folded into quarters diagonally.

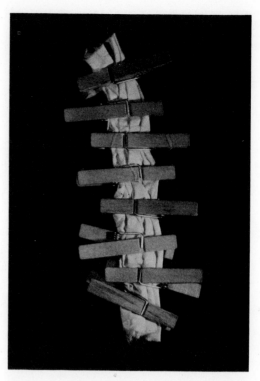

Fold the cloth in half across. Gather it into a roll. Place pegs over it, first on the left and then on the right side.

Dyed effect.

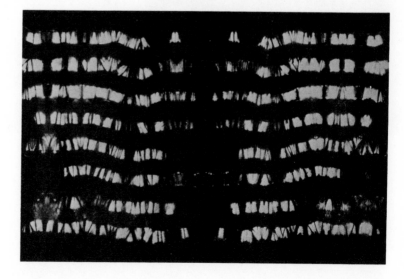

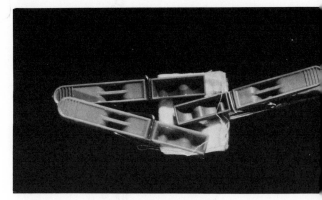

As on previous page except that the cloth is folded into *pleats*.

Stripe pattern after one dyeing.

Fold cloth into four lengthways and then into four across. Add three pegs.

Result after dyeing.

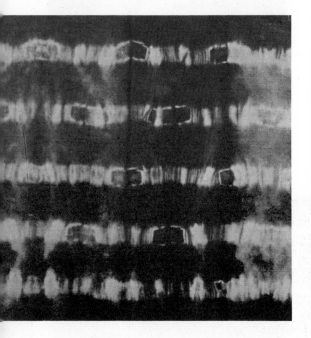

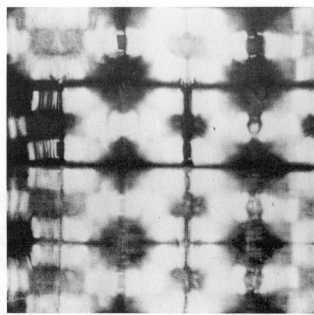

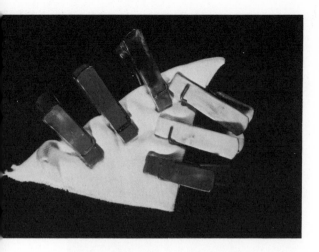

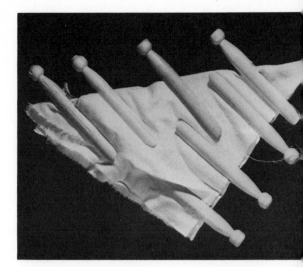

Fold a square of cloth into quarters and then across to form a triangle.
Add pegs along the folded edges.

Circular pattern produced after one dyeing.

Fold a square of cloth into quarters and then across into a triangle. Add larger pegs to the folded edges, parallel to the bottom edge.

Effect after one dyeing. These larger pegs produce a different type of pattern from the spring pegs.

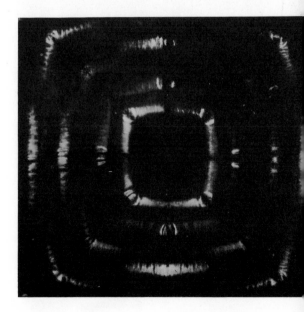

Fold a square of cloth into quarters, then across into a triangle. Fold in half to make a smaller triangle. Add large pegs as shown.

Dyed design.

This is a useful plastic clip peg. Use for cold dyeing only.

Fold cloth lengthways. Put clip pegs across, first from the left side and then from the right. Sample shows effect after dyeing.

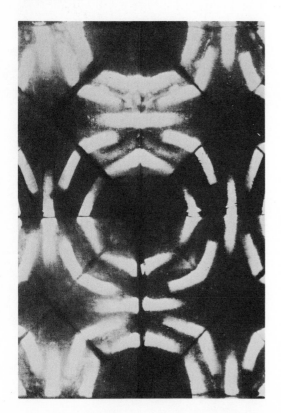

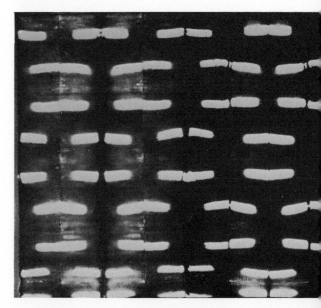

Fold a square of cloth into quarters and then across into a triangle. Put clip pegs along the folded edges. Result after dyeing.

Fold cloth in half lengthways, then across into four. Add two bulldog clips as shown.

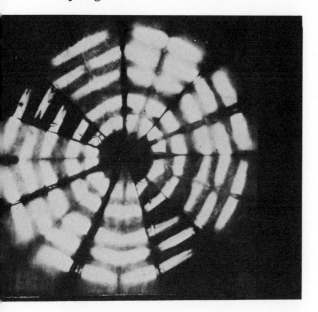

Effect after one dyeing.

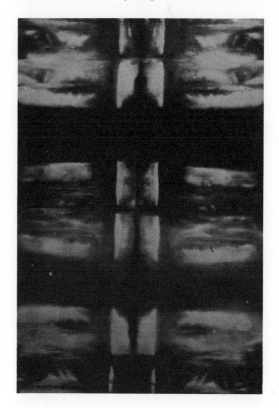

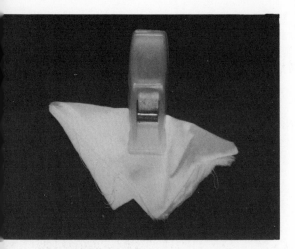

Effect after folding cloth into pleats lengthways and adding pegs. Undo after the first dyeing. Re-fold and add pegs. Dye the second colour.

Fold cloth into four lengthways then into half across. Fold diagonally. Add a large plastic clip.

Design after dyeing.

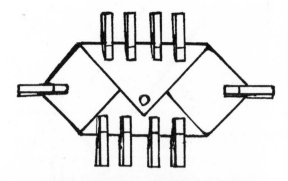

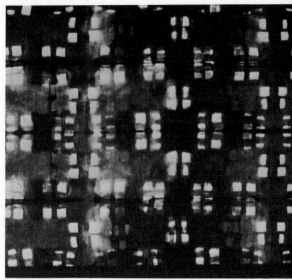

Effect after folding the cloth lengthways and then across. Add pegs to all sides. Undo, then re-fold, and put pegs on again before dyeing the second colour.

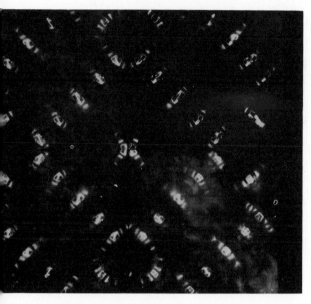

Effect after folding a square of cloth into quarters. Fold the centre and the opposite corners in towards each other. Add four pegs each side and one at each corner. Dye one colour.

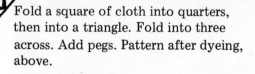

Fold a square of cloth into quarters, then into a triangle. Fold into three across. Add pegs. Pattern after dyeing, above.

Fold the cloth into four lengthways, then
wrap round polythene as shown. Add
pegs.

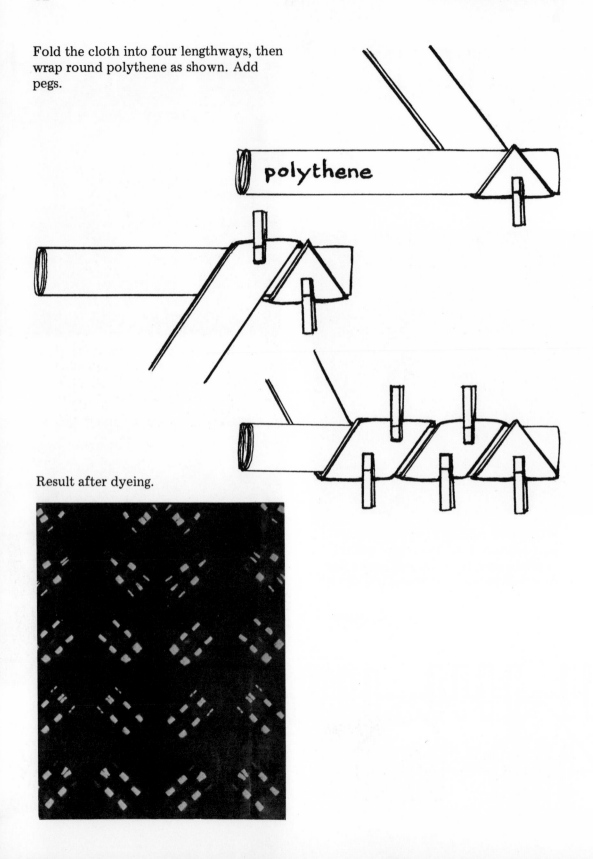

Result after dyeing.

Fold a square of cloth in half diagonally, then make into pleats across. Add five bulldog clips.

Result after dyeing.

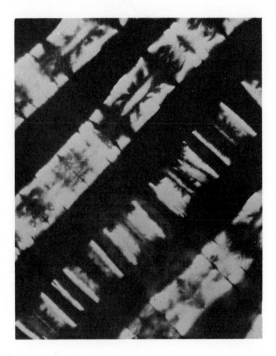

Fold a small piece of cloth into four across. Turn down one of the corners and add small clips.

Dyed effect.

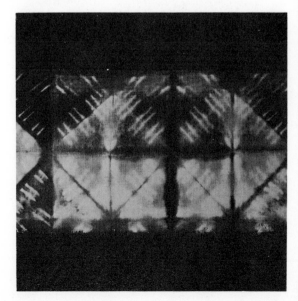

RUBBER BANDS AND RINGS

With many methods you can get very good and varied effects by using rubber bands and rings in place of the usual binding. They are fairly cheap to buy and come in various sizes and thicknesses. They are splendid for children and beginners as they are quick and easy to put on the sample.

The following hints may prove helpful:

Use the very fine rubber rings for cold dyeing only. They have a nasty habit of snapping and shooting off the sample when put in very hot dye. Do not overstretch these fine rings or they will break. Rather add an extra ring to finish off the binding. If they persist in breaking try working with double identical rings instead of the one.

To vary the dyed texture put wide bands and narrow rings in different parts of the same sample.

You will get a more interesting texture if the rubber rings or bands are arranged in a criss-cross manner. To do this, slip the rubber ring round the sample and hold it in the left hand. Put two or three fingers of the right hand inside the rest of the ring to spread it out. Keep the fingers apart while turning the hand over and back again. This makes the rubber ring cross over itself as it binds along the sample, producing the desired criss-cross effect.

The wider bands are much tougher and can be used in very hot dye without fear of their breaking.

Sometimes you cannot apply the rings and bands to the sample tightly enough to produce a good resist. To remedy this insert part of a matchstick or something similar under a loop of the rubber ring.

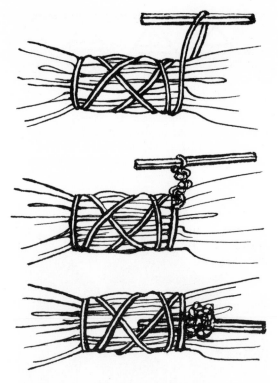

Twist the matchstick round like a corkscrew. This takes up the slack ring and twists it into a "neck". Push the matchstick containing the twist of rubber ring under the binding already made. Leave it there while the sample is dyed.

If it is necessary to join on another ring in the middle of a length of binding:

1. Slip a loop of ring No 2 under No 1.

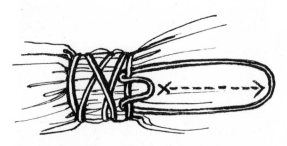

2. Pull the remainder of ring No 2 right through the No 2 loop.

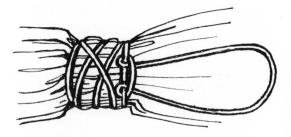

3. Tighten up the slip knot thus made and continue with the binding.

To undo the rubber rings after dyeing, insert a matchstick or a fine metal object inside the ring and heave it over the sample. The rest should come undone easily. To bind small objects into the cloth such as stones, use the very small fine rubber rings.

To make some cheap rubber bands collect old rubber inner tubes from bicycles, rubber gloves, etc. and cut them across into parallel slices.

Marbling

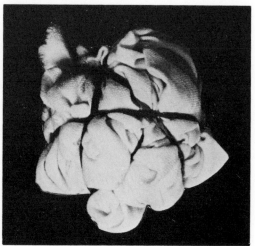

Bunch up the cloth into a ball in the hands. Put rubber rings around it in all directions.

Result when the sample is re-tied and dyed a second colour.

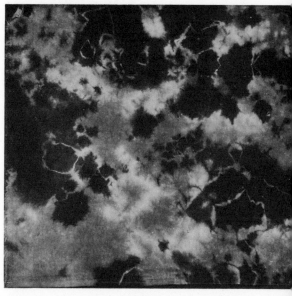

Bands of texture

Fold cloth in half lengthways, then gather and add a rubber band.

This produces two bands of texture because it was folded. Result, overleaf.

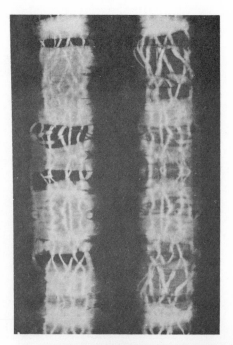

This gives a design of three textured stripes. For a longer piece of cloth with more stripes, add extra rubber rings or bands at intervals.

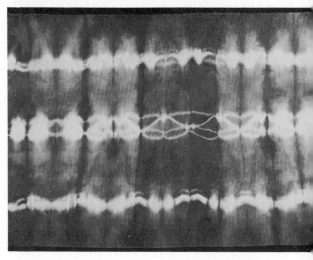

STICKS, CORKS AND COTTON REELS

Use any small flat stick such as a lollypop stick, a popsicle stick or an ice cream stick.

Put a stick under a small square of cloth. Criss-cross some rubber rings along it.

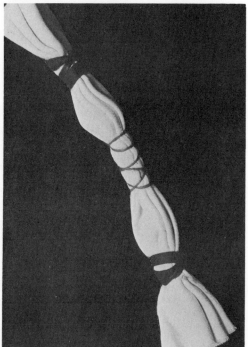

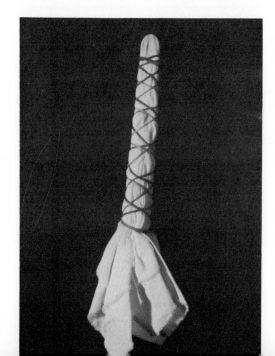

Fold cloth in half across. Make into pleats across. Put a thick rubber band at each end and spread out a finer rubber ring criss-crossed, in the middle of the bundle.

This gives a circle design.

Using half sticks, arrange four in a square of cloth. Add rubber rings as above.

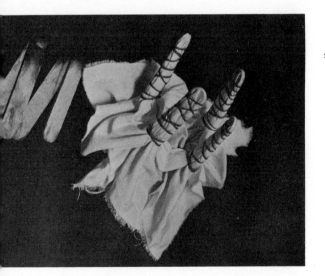

To make the design below put one stick in the centre of the cloth and a bundle of three matchsticks (tied together) at each corner. Criss-cross with rubber rings.

When dyed this gives a circle pattern for each half stick.

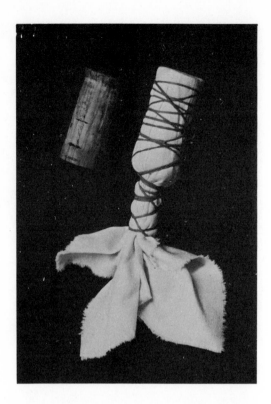

Pleat or gather the cloth lengthways.
Wrap it round a cotton reel. Add several
rubber rings.

Dyed texture.

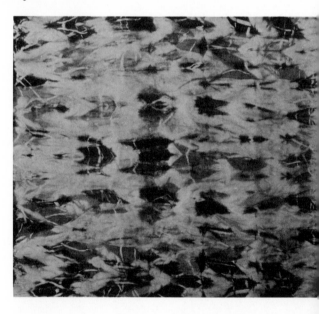

Wrap your cloth over a cork. Criss-cross
rubber rings around and underneath the
cork.

Effect after one dyeing.

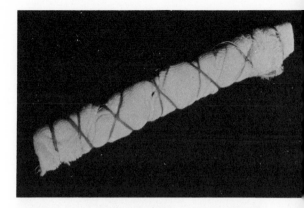

Gather your cloth round several cotton reels. Add rubber rings and rubber bands in between, and around the cotton reels.

Pattern after one dyeing.

Fold a small piece of cloth into a narrow strip lengthways. Roll it diagonally around a small stick. To begin, clip the cloth on to the stick with a peg. Remove this after adding rubber rings along the sample.

After the first dyeing. Untie the sample, re-arrange the cloth and wind it on the stick as before.

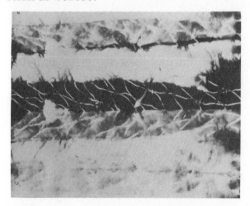

Pattern after the second dyeing.

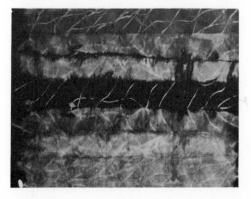

For this design, fold the cloth into
quarters. Put a rubber ring just below
the centre point and another below the
opposite corners. Effect after one dyeing.

1 Skirt in heavy furnishing cotton.
Sewing and binding method.

2 Sarong dress in sheeting. The material
was marked out with circles before being
made up. By courtesy of *Woman*.

3 (*Above, opposite*) Four cotton ties –
various methods. By courtesy of Dylon.

4 (*Opposite left*) T-Shirt – centre back and
centre front of garment were folded so
that they were on the outside and parallel
rows of stitches made from both folds
sloping diagonally from centre towards
the top and lower edge.

5 (*Opposite right*) Matching tie and
handkerchief – folding and binding
method.

6 (*Above*) *Pop Star* – made from an old
cardigan with frayed knitted fabric for
hair. The clothes are small pieces of
tie-and-dye.

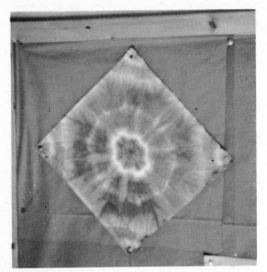

7 & 8 Samples dyed by six- and seven-year-olds from Beacontree Heath Infants' School.

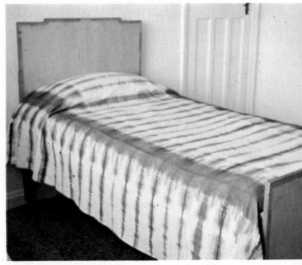

10 Cotton sheeting bedspread dyed in stripes of one colour.

9 Lengths of fabric dyed in chevron pattern in three colours.

2 KNOTTING

Very fine fabrics such as muslin, lawn, voile, thin poplin, cambric, jap silk, silk chiffon and georgette, etc., are most successful for these methods.

Most knotted patterns are improved when dyed a second or third colour. To do this, untie the knots after dyeing the first colour. Rinse and dry. Tie the knots up again in the same place as before. Wet out and dye the second colour. Repeat for a third colour.

A LENGTH OF CLOTH

Fold this in half lengthways. Twist it and tie it into knots at intervals. Put rubber rings on the knots if necessary.

After one dyeing. Undo the sample then tie up again as before.

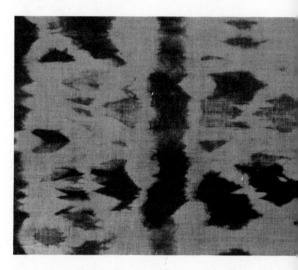

After the second dyeing.

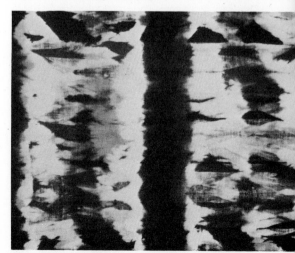

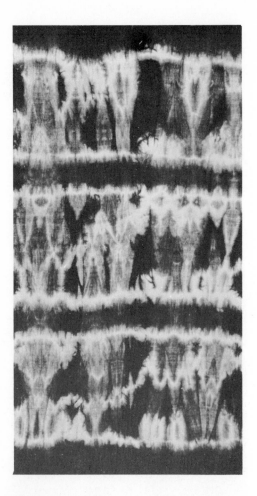

First dyeing—sample dyed dry. Second dyeing—sample wetted out before dyeing.

A SQUARE OF CLOTH

1. Pick up the centre point of a square or rectangle of fine cloth. Twist it and tie it into a knot. Tie knots at each of the four corners.

Three knots tied on a length of cloth as before.

Effect after two dyeings, undoing the sample and re-tying in between.

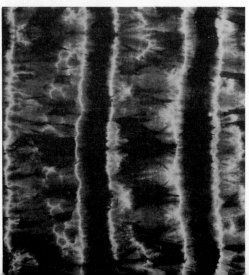

After one dyeing.

2. Tie a knot in the centre of a square. Pull out the centre tuft long enough to tie a second knot above the first one. Dye two colours.

4. Tie a knot in the centre of a square of cloth and pull out a long tuft at the centre. Bind this tuft with rubber rings (or thread).

Dye the tuft a different colour from the rest of the sample.

3. Tie a knot in the centre of a square of fine cloth. Put a binding or rubber rings on each of the four corners. After the sample has been dyed and before undoing it, the corners only can be dipped in a darker coloured dye. The corners can be bound after the whole sample has been dyed the first colour.

Knotting is an easy and satisfactory method of obtaining a pattern if undoing the knots can be dealt with. For children it is best to aim at a knot which they can undo themselves. Then to help give a satisfactory resist, twist several rubber rings around each knot. Always wet out the sample before dyeing.

If the knots are still difficult to untie try:

1. Undoing the knots while the sample is in water.

2. Leave until it is bone dry. Then twist the cloth on either side of the knot back into it as if undoing a screw. This often loosens the knot enough so that you can gradually pull it undone.

UNDOING KNOTS USING GADGETS

Another completely different approach to make the knots easier to undo is to insert some object in the knot itself. Put it inside the fold of the knot just before the final tightening-up. After dyeing, it is taken out, leaving the knot loose and thus easier to untie. Almost any small gadget that does not spoil the pattern will do: half matchsticks (two or three),

For an **all-over** pattern, pick up points of cloth at intervals on a length of fine cloth. Twist and tie the points into knots. After the first dyeing, rinse and untie. Dry.

Tie it up again as before and dye a second colour.

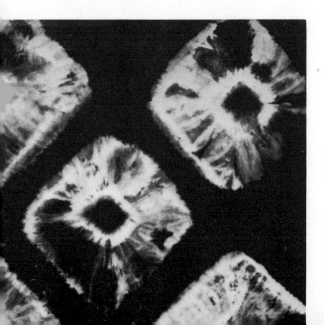

bits broken from small sticks, milk tops made into rolls, tiny bits of wood. You will think of many other suitable things. The important thing is they must stay in place while the sample is being dyed and they must be easy to pull out afterwards.

Place a piece of rope on the cloth and tie it into a knot along with the cloth. To

untie after dyeing, ease the rope round the outside of the knot and it should pull right out, leaving the knot loose.

Prepare some string loops by tying together both ends of some pieces of string 7-10 ins long. You need two loops for each knot. Thread the two loops on the cloth. Then tie the knot so that there is a loop of string on either side of the central tuft of cloth. This method of undoing is easier if the sample is bone dry. To untie the knot pull the two string loops away from each other until the knot loosens.

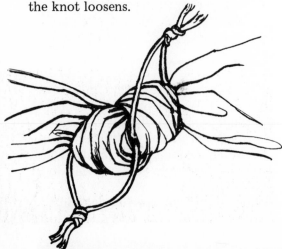

Any kind of metal or plastic ring can be threaded on the cloth beforehand—two rings for each knot of course—and used in the same way as the string.

CLOTH ROLLED ON ROPE AND KNOTTED

Fine cloth is best for this method. The rope should be slightly longer than the cloth. In the diagrams in this section, the direction of the dyed stripe is shown by a dotted line.

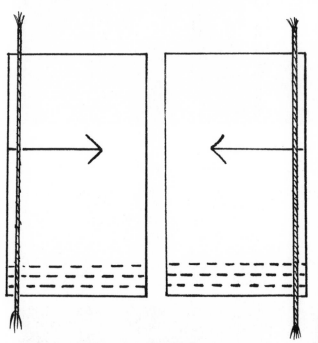

Straight rolling on single cloth

Place the rope along the left side of the cloth. Cover the edge of the cloth over the rope and roll both over to the right side. There is now a tube of cloth with the rope down the centre. Tie the tube into knots at intervals. Dye the first colour. Rinse, untie and unroll. Repeat the whole process, beginning with the rope on the right side. Roll across towards the left side. The cloth that was inside the roll for the first dyeing is now on the outside. Tie the tube into knots as before. Dye the second colour.

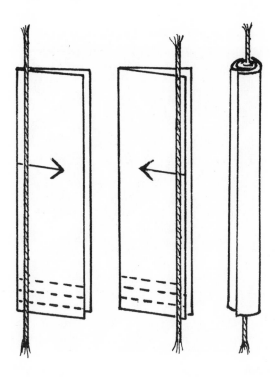

Straight rolling on folded cloth

Dyed design.

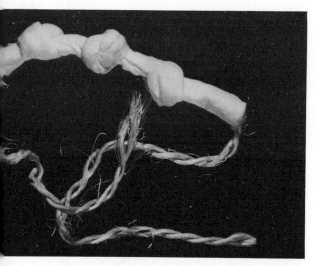

Fold cloth in half lengthways. Place the rope along the folded edge. Roll and tie as above. Dye, rinse, untie and unroll it. Turn the sample over. Place the rope along the open edges and roll towards the fold. Tie as before. Dye the second colour.

Diagonal rolling on single cloth

Place the rope across one of the four corners of the cloth. Roll the rope and the cloth diagonally across to the opposite corner. Tie the roll into knots. Dye the first colour. Rinse, untie and unroll.

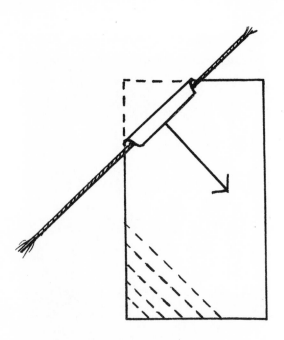

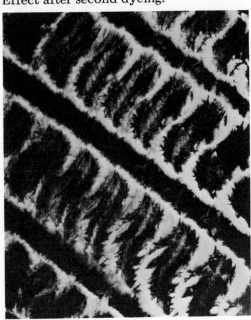

Effect after second dyeing.

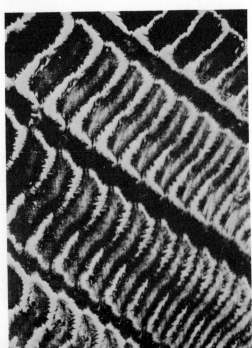

Effect after first dyeing. Repeat but
this time place the rope across the corner
that came on the outside of the roll. Roll
across to the opposite corner and tie
into knots as before. Dye the second
colour.

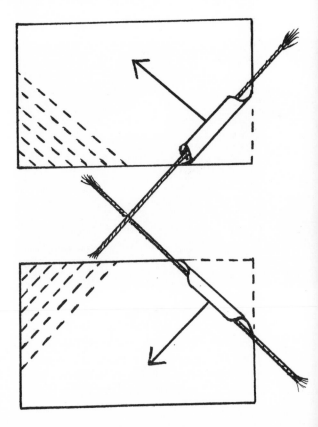

For a pattern sloping in the opposite direction, begin the rolling from the adjacent corner as shown on page 48.

To get a trellis effect, roll from corner A for the first colour. Untie, then roll from corner B for the second colour.

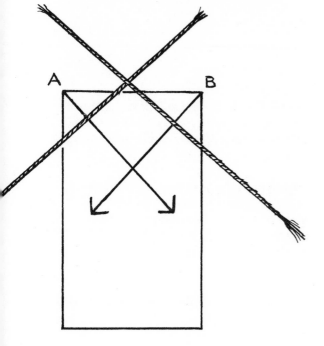

Two ropes can be used as below. This also applies to diagonal rolling but only when the two ropes can be placed at opposite corners.

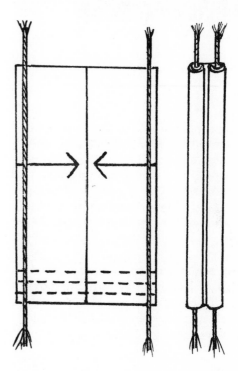

Diagonal rolling on double cloth

Use very fine cloth for the best results. Fold the cloth in half lengthways, or in half across, then follow instructions for diagonal rolling on single cloth above. If the cloth is very fine such as muslin or silk chiffon it is possible to fold it into quarters before rolling up and knotting. Pin in place while rolling, but remove the pins before the dyeing. This gives a pattern in the form of an "X". See diagrams on pages 107-109 and 157.

3
BINDING

Some people are able to bind a sample with thread but find it difficult to make the fastening-on and fastening-off knots. The following methods should solve their problem. Also, the great advantage is that after dyeing, the binding can be unwound very easily, and saved to use again.

Teachers may wish to avoid the use of scissors. If lengths of thread, string or raffia of a convenient size are cut beforehand and given out to each child, there is no need for scissors.

BINDING WITHOUT TYING KNOTS

To fasten on the thread:

A. Place the thumb on the cloth where the binding is to be made. Put the thread under the thumb (usually the left thumb) allowing about 2-3 ins of thread to hang down loose.

While the thumb is pressed on the small piece of thread (a pin marks the spot), wrap the other end round the sample several times. Pull it tight. Release the small piece of thread and turn it upwards.

B. Bind once round the sample to secure the end of thread.

C. Finish the binding in this area.

To fasten off the thread:

When the binding is finished wrap the thread round the sample once or twice more.

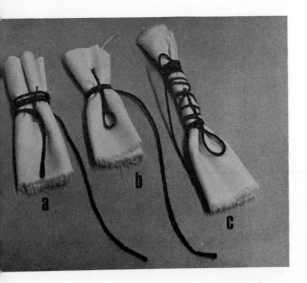

Put a small rubber ring round the end of the binding to hold it tight.

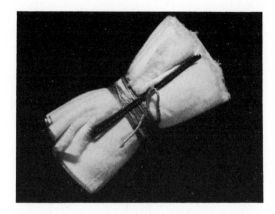

A hair grip or similar small grip can be used instead of the rubber ring. Push the hair grip over the end of thread and down over the other binding. Paper clips can be used too but sometimes they become tangled with the binding.

BINDING USING SLIP KNOTS

Everyone who intends to do much binding should master one of the slip-knot methods and should learn to do it easily and quickly.

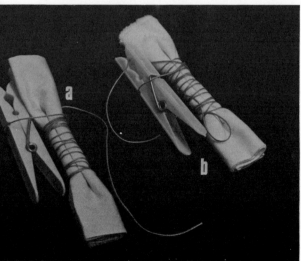

A When the binding is finished, cut the thread with 6 ins to spare. Place a spring peg alongside the sample. Wrap the binding thread round the sample and peg together.

B Bring the cut end of thread over the front of the sample, and clip it in the peg. Pull the peg with the end of thread down underneath the last round of binding. Remove the peg. Pull the end of thread so that it grips tautly.

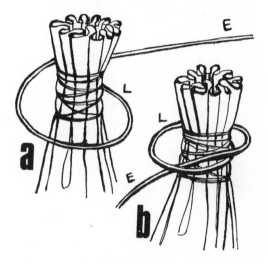

1a Finish the binding. Leave the last round loose (L).

1b Slip the working end of thread E underneath L.

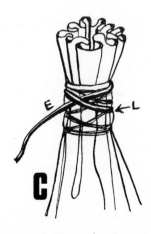

1c Pull E taut over the existing binding. The loop L now grips E so tightly that it will hold fast during dyeing.

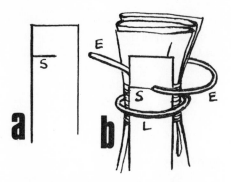

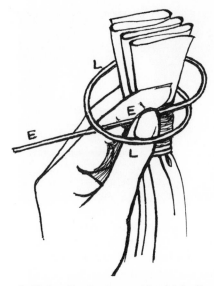

2a Besides the peg method shown in the photographs, other gadgets can be used to pull E through the last round of binding L. Cut a narrow strip of fine cardboard and make a slit S near the top of the left side.

2b Take the last round of binding over it and slide E in the slit S.

3 Take the last round of binding L over the left thumb and forefinger. Bring the end of thread E round and place between them. Lower the thumb and forefinger holding E below L. Tighten E.

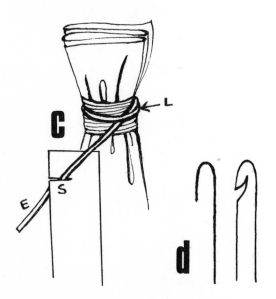

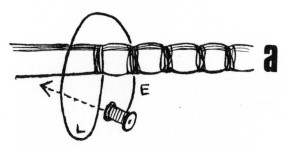

2c Pull down the cardboard containing E below L. Tighten E and then remove the cardboard.

2d In the same way use a piece of bent wire, pipe cleaners, or a crochet hook.

4a For a long sample with slip knots in the centre. At each binding make a loop L.

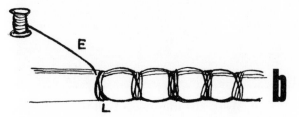

4b Thread the reel with the working end of thread E through the loop L. Tighten E.

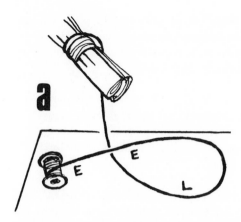

5a This is an easy method for children. Point the sample downwards and make a loop of thread L on the desk or table in an anti-clockwise direction.

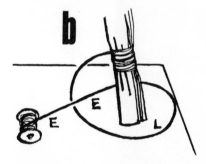

5b Place the sample (pointing downwards) in the centre of loop L.

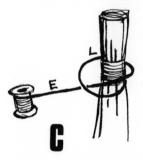

5c Lift up the sample with the loop L round it. Pull the thread E taut.

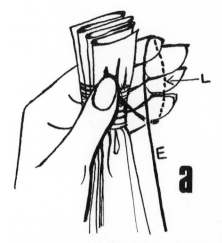

6a Wrap the working end of thread E down and round the back of the fingers of the left hand in an anti-clockwise direction.

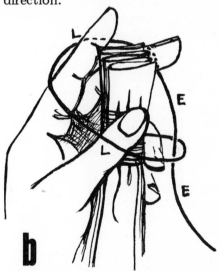

6b With the right hand pick up the loop L thus made and place it over the sample so that E is underneath the loop L.

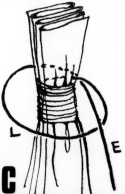

6c Pull E taut.

When the slip knot is made by any method it should hold in place throughout the dyeing, without slackening.

To undo a binding where a slip knot has been used, find the end of thread and pull as if to *unwind* the binding. As soon as it yields to this pull, take it from under the last round of binding thread holding it down. You can then unwind the whole binding. There should be no need to use scissors with the risk of cutting holes in the sample. The thread can be wound on to a piece of cardboard as it comes off the sample and can be used again.

Binding is important because it influences the type of pattern created. There are three main sorts of binding.

1. A solid bound band which keeps out all or most of the dye in that area. Strong thick thread, string or raffia are excellent for this method. Make the binding so compact that the cloth does not show through.

2. Criss-cross or open binding. This gives an interesting texture on the pattern. Fine grained to medium fabrics bound with cotton or linen thread give more precise and richer textures. These grip into the cloth better than a string or coarser thread. Use the coarse as well as the fine thread if a variety of texture is called for.

3. Line binding. This is a very narrow, firm binding made on the cloth giving the effect of a white line on the pattern. Use strong fine thread for this type of binding.

With all binding the "fastening on" and a "fastening off" are important. The fastening on can be done without a knot

(see page 50) or you can wrap the thread round the sample several times and tie the two ends together. Continue binding with the longer thread.

The "fastening off". Tie the two ends of thread together if they are near each other. Otherwise finish with a slip knot using one of the methods shown in the diagrams.

The method for tightening up rubber rings can also be used for binding that is too slack (see page 34).

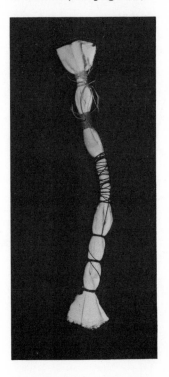

This bound sample shows:

1. Area bound solidly with raffia.

2. A solid band of binding, using thick thread fastened off with a slip knot.

3. Criss-cross binding with finer thread.

4. Three line bindings fastened off with a rubber ring.

A very good cheap binding is made by cutting old nylon stockings in a slightly spiral direction in a strip about ½-1 inch wide. This forms a narrow tube, like a rope if it is stretched after being cut. Wrap the cut stocking on a piece of cardboard. It can be used over and over again.

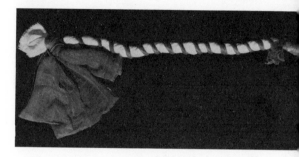

Dyed sample showing effects of the various bindings.

Stretch out a very fine nylon stocking to use as a binding round a bundle of cloth.

Dyed effect.

ECONOMICAL BINDINGS

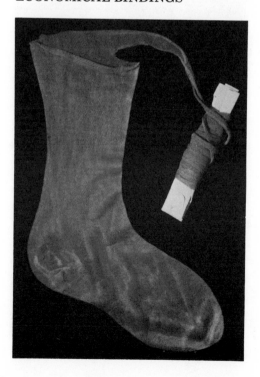

When binding material is short or too expensive, use tape, strips of cloth torn from old garments and tear off narrow hems or seams from old handkerchiefs or pillow cases. They give very pleasing results.

A hem torn from an old garment used as binding.

Dyed effect.

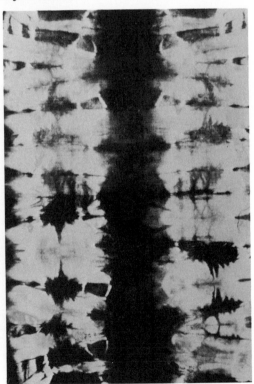

BINDING WITH POLYTHENE

To make a more solid binding, or one on a very large sample, polythene can be combined with rubber rings or bands. Roll a strip of polythene, or a polythene bag into a narrow tube. Wrap it round and round the sample.

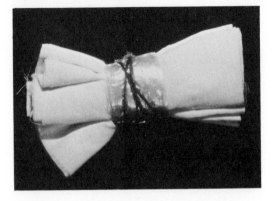

Hold it in place with a rubber ring or band, or a binding of string.

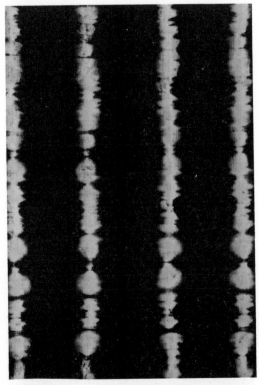

Dyed stripe effect. This binding can be

repeated at intervals. The bands of polythene can be narrow or wide. It is a good means of blocking out large areas of a sample if you wish them to remain undyed.

DYED THREAD AND STRING FOR BINDING

Use thread or string saved from a previous dyeing—it often leaves traces of its colour on the new sample. Or, dye thread and string in household or direct dyes and dry without rinsing. This should definitely transfer colour to the new sample.

MARBLING

A small piece. Place the cloth flat on the table or desk. Bunch it into a ball, tuck the edges in and add binding in all directions until it is quite solid (see page 35). Wet out before dyeing. For the

second colour, untie the sample. Bunch it up again and bind as before. Wet out and dye. Rinse and untie.

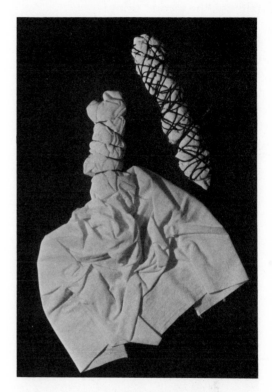

A larger length. Place the cloth flat on the table. Turn under about 3 ins of cloth along each side. Begin the bunching up on the right side of the sample. Pick up small tufts across the cloth. Hold them in the left hand while a loose binding is added. Pick up another row of tufts parallel with the first about 6 or 8 ins further along the cloth. Push them up against the first row and add a little more binding, enough to hold the folds together. Continue to pick up parallel rows of tufts in this way, 6-8 ins apart and to put on a loose binding until the whole of the cloth is formed into a loose "sausage". Then cover the whole of it with tighter firmer binding until a smaller more compact roll is formed. Wet out and dye the first colour. Rinse and untie. Dry.

If more texture is needed bunch it up as before. This time pick up tufts of cloth in the areas that need more colour. Bind it up again into a compact roll, wet out and dye the second colour.

small stick to push up the cloth into a point. Add binding or rubber rings, near the point for a small circle, further away for a larger one.

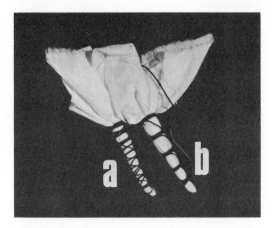

A. Bind diagonally up to the tip. Then pull the thread taut against the left thumb to grip the point, to prevent the binding from slipping off during dyeing. Bind back down the circle over the first layer of binding, pulling the thread tightly. Finish with a slip knot.

B. Concentric circles. Make line bindings at intervals on the point of cloth. You can work from the tip, downwards or from the outside of the circle up towards the central point.

Dyed effects.

A length of cloth of several yards may need a third dyeing to get an interesting texture spread over it evenly. When the tied-up bundle is very solid or bulky it can be dyed dry, to allow the dye to penetrate more. When dyeing several colours, they can be in complete contrast or in harmony. The same colour can be dyed over again, to build up an even texture.

BOUND CIRCLES

Suitable for all kinds of cloth and all sizes. Pick up a point of cloth and for each circle smooth it down like a closed umbrella. Use a pencil, matchstick or

A cluster of concentric circles varying in size.

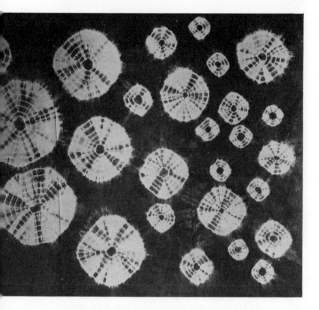

The dyed texture within the circle depends on how much binding there is, how tight it is and on the thickness of the thread.

SPOTS

Fine-medium cloth. Any length.

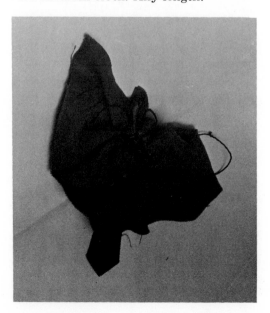

Top: Pick up a very small point of cloth with the thumb and forefinger or with a needle. Tie the fine binding thread on the cloth just below the point and make a firm line binding. Secure with a slip knot, then take the binding thread across to bind the next spot.

Bottom: For a wider band of texture add more binding.

Dyed effects. *Top*: a narrow resist ring. *Bottom*: a larger spot with more resist texture.

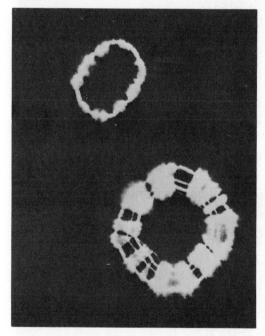

Plan the design beforehand. Put pencil dots on the cloth where each spot is to be made. Very fine cloth may be folded in half and the spots tied on double cloth. This saves time. Some of the spots on the double cloth could be tied on one side and some on the other side, so that both halves of the sample are dyed evenly.

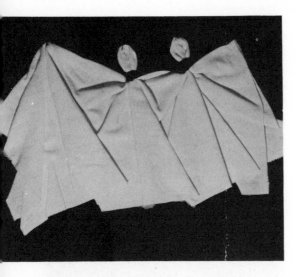

For rows of spots draw the lines in
pencil or make creases on the cloth. Pick
up points of cloth along each line or
crease. Add binding just below the
points. Make a slip knot. Take the thread
along to bind the next spot.

Lines of dyed spots.

How to tie spots over an area of cloth
without using slip knots. Pick up points
of cloth at regular intervals on a pin or
needle. Put a binding thread just below
the point—take the thread along to bind
the next spot.

Effect after the first dyeing. Untie the
sample. Pick up points of cloth
haphazardly and add binding.

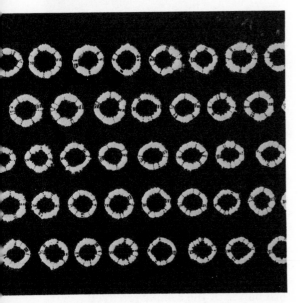

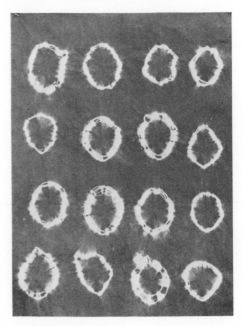

Effect after second dyeing.

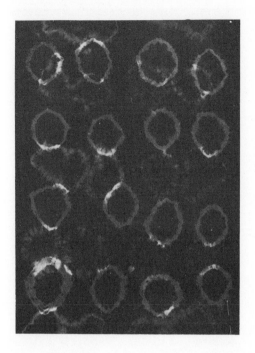

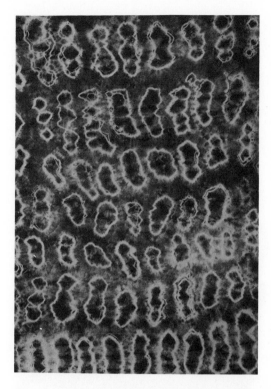

MULTISPOTS

Pick up two or more "tufts" of cloth on a needle and bind them together as one spot. Remove the needle. Take the thread along to bind the next multispot.

Sample showing how the multispot can be used for an all-over pattern.

A very effective pattern for cold water dyes is as follows:

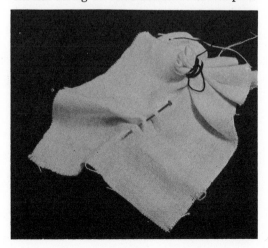

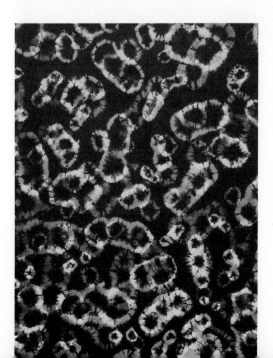

1. Draw ovals on a cloth all sloping to the right. Make them of varying sizes. According to the size of each one, pick up one, two, three or four tufts of cloth within the oval. Bind each oval separately. Wet out. Dye the first colour in a reactive dye. Rinse and untie. Dry.

2. Repeat the whole process but this time draw all the ovals sloping the other way, to the left. Pick up the points of cloth and bind each oval. Wet out. Dye the sample in a reactive dye of contrasting colour for the maximum effect. For instance, red/blue, orange/blue.

STRIPES

Stripes down the cloth

Small or large pieces of cloth.

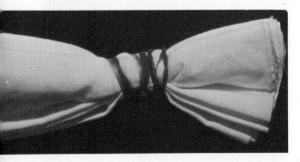

Fold the cloth in half lengthways. Gather it across into a bundle. Put a rubber band or some binding round the middle. Wet out or dye dry. Open up the folds of cloth so that the dye penetrates up as far as the binding.

Dyed stripe effect.

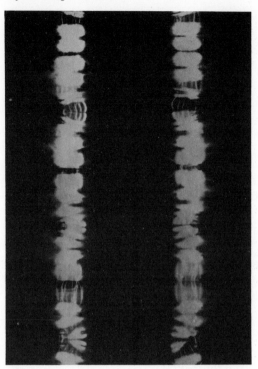

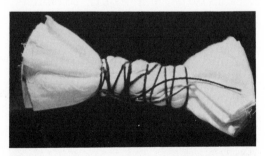

This sample is the same as above except that the cloth was made into pleats after folding in half lengthways. Add a wider band of binding.

Result is two resist stripes.

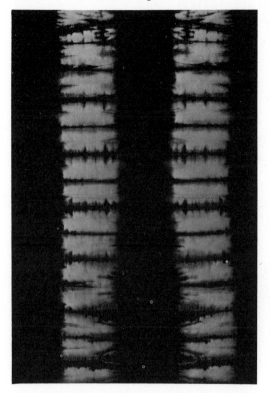

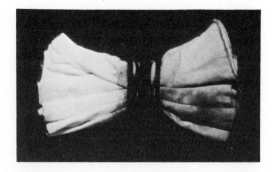

Fold sample into three lengthways, then pleat across to form a bundle. Put binding round the middle. Place one side in the dye as far up as the binding. After dyeing rinse.

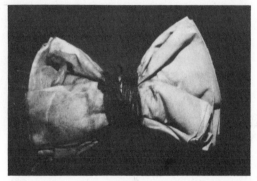

For more stripes fold the cloth into four, six or eight lengthways, then pleat across into a bundle. Put binding round the middle. This sample shows the dyed effect when the cloth is folded eight times. The two sides of the tied-up bundle can be dyed different colours.

Place the other half in dye of a different colour up to the binding.

Folded as above. Dyed different colours on either side of the binding.

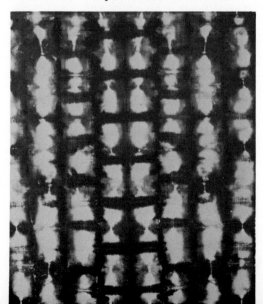

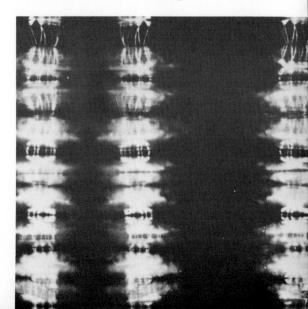

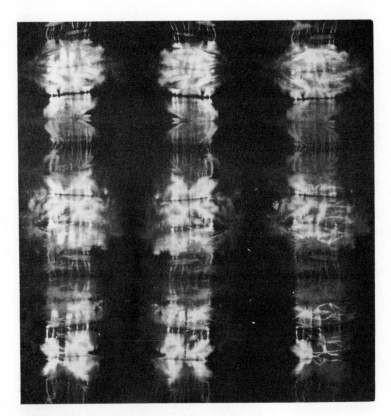

Folded and dyed as on previous page.
Then untied. Fold up the cloth as before
but into three across, at right angles to
the first folds. This produces stripes crossing over the first layer, making a plaid
pattern.

Stripes across the cloth or rope tying

This method involves a great many line
bindings. The following hints may help
to speed up the operation.

Line bindings are best done with strong,
fine cotton or linen thread. They are
made by concentrating the fine binding
thread into a narrow area, then leaving
a definite gap of cloth in between each
binding. Strong machine thread, if pulled
gently is good on fine fabrics. Strong
thread as used by tailors, No 10 and
No 24 and button-hole thread are ideal.

Terylene and nylon thread can be used if
they are not "stretchy". The very fine
threads snap if they are "jerked" but
will withstand firm gentle pulling. Use a
slip knot to finish each individual
binding. Then take the thread along
without cutting it, to make the next
binding. Try to form the habit of
pressing the left thumb nail firmly on the
spot where the binding is to be made.

1. How to work from the left or the
lower edge of the sample. Press the left
thumb nail on the thread at the spot for
the first binding. Fasten on the thread.

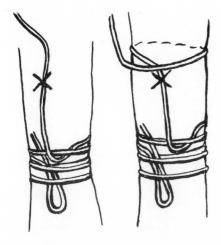

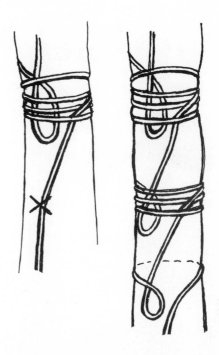

Finish off the first line binding. Make a slip knot if necessary. Take the thread along beyond the last binding and place the left thumb nail on it where you require the next binding (marked X on diagram). Make sure that when the thread is wrapped round the sample it passes *over* the bit held under the thumb nail. By crossing over it like this, the binding is secured and will hold firm. Finish off the second binding and continue along the sample in this way, ending with a slip knot.

2. How to work from the right or the top edge of the sample. Press the left thumb nail on the thread at the spot for the first binding. Fasten on and make the first binding. Make a slip knot if necessary. Move the thread down. Place the left thumb nail on it where the next binding is required (marked X on diagram). Bring the thread up by the side of the thumb (which is still pressed on the thread) and bind round the sample several times, just beyond the tip of the thumb nail. Tighten the binding. Then take the thumb away. There should be a small loop of thread below the binding. Leave it. Finish off the binding and make a slip knot. Repeat this for every binding, down the sample.

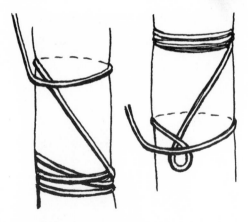

3. With careful practice and on non-slippery cloth it is possible to make line bindings without a slip knot in between. When each binding is finished pull the thread gently and diagonally across the bundle, to the spot for the next binding. Press the left thumb nail on the thread and proceed as above. It is most essential that the first round of each line of binding grips the diagonal thread so securely in place that it cannot move or slacken.

Fold the cloth in half lengthways. Make into accordion pleats lengthways. Add binding at intervals, lines, bands or areas of criss-cross binding, or a mixture of all kinds. Use a continuous binding thread and fasten off with a slip knot.

Dyed stripe.

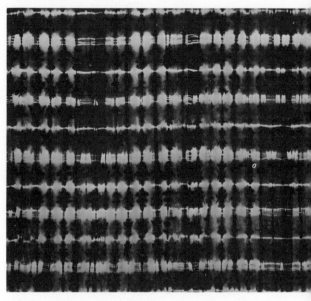

Before dyeing the second or third colours add to or change the position of the bindings.

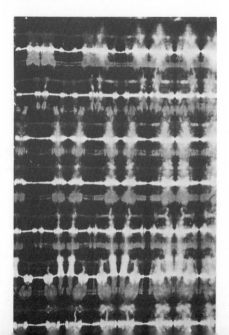

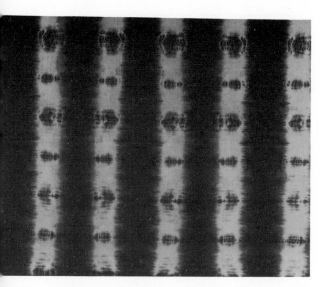

This shows fine cloth pleated into accordion pleats with bands of binding to give broader stripes.

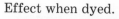

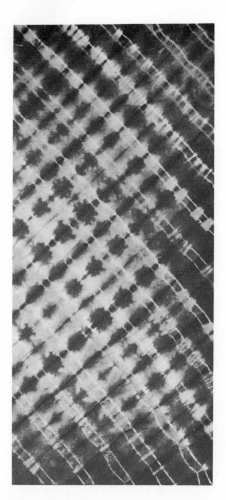

Fold and pleat as above. At one end of the sample bindings are narrow and they get wider towards the lower edge.

Effect when dyed.

To make diagonal stripes the accordion pleats run diagonally across the cloth.

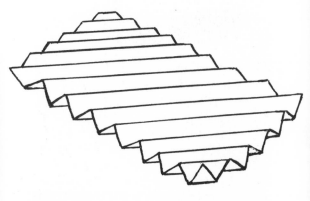

For zig-zags, fold the cloth in half lengthways for one chevron, into three,

four or more thicknesses lengthways for
more chevrons or zig-zags. Then make
accordion pleats across the folded cloth
diagonally as in diagram. In all cases, add
bindings at intervals.

Dyed results.

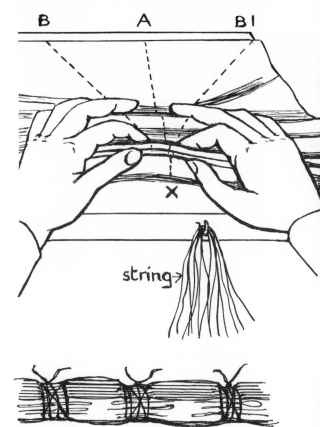

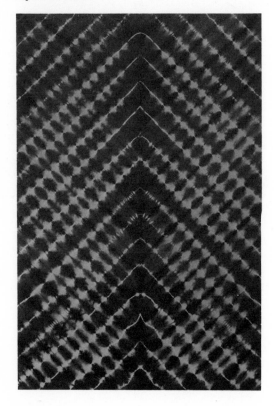

**Dyeing stripes across several yards of
cloth**

Method 1 can be carried out by one
person or as a class project. Fold the
cloth in half lengthways and place on a
flat smooth surface, such as a table. Have
ready cut a supply of pieces of string
about 10 ins long. Place the folded edge
of cloth nearest you and begin there.
Creases can be made in the cloth or lines
drawn at right angles to the fold as guide
lines if necessary. Hold the cloth, with
both hands resting on the table. "Nibble"

up small pieces of cloth with the two big
fingers. As these small pleats are formed,
grip them between the thumbs and fore-
fingers. Work right across the cloth from
the folded edge to the selvedge edges X
to A. Pick up a piece of string and make a
binding round the pleated area. Repeat
this pleating across the cloth and binding,
at intervals.

For a class project children can stand
about two feet apart along the table.
Each child pleats the cloth across where
he or she stands. Another group of
children can tie on the binding thread or
string while the first group holds the
pleated cloth. At this stage it is a good
plan to tug both ends of the pleated
cloth to even up some of the
irregularities. Extra rows of pleats can be
made across the cloth, in between the

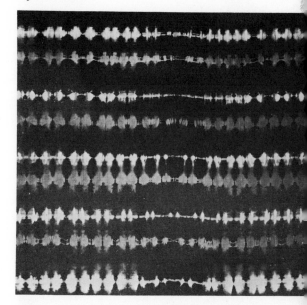

Dyed result.

existing ones. Bind these. Add more
bindings before the first, second or even
third dyeing.

Method 2. This is basically the same as
Method 1 in the way some children pleat
the cloth across and others add the
binding. The only difference is, that it is
done without a table. The children doing
the pleating stand in a row close together.
They all hold the folded edge of cloth
and then proceed to make the pleats
across. The others hold up the selvedge
edges and have the string ready for
binding on their arm.

Diagonal stripes can be made on single
cloth in a similar manner. The direction
of the diagonals BX or BIX must be
drawn, or a crease made across the cloth
before the pleating is done.

A chevron pattern can also be made.
Fold the cloth in half lengthways for one
chevron, into four for two chevrons.
Place the cloth on the table, mark out
the diagonal guide lines and proceed as
for the diagonal stripes above.

Cloth can be pleated in any of the ways
shown in the reference diagrams on
page 157.

4
BINDING OBJECTS INTO CLOTH

This shows three small stones bound above one larger stone.

The dyed effect.

This method is within the scope of most people because rubber rings and bands can be used as well as binding for securing the objects in the cloth. It depends for its pattern interest on the variety of things available, how they are tied in and the way they are arranged.

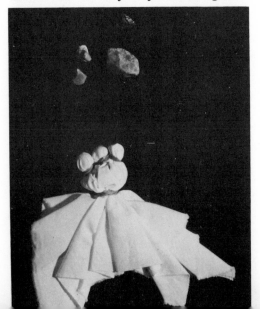

Have a large box for storing any likely objects for future use. Get busy right away. Here are some things to start saving:

Stones of all shapes and sizes, all sorts of corks, plastic bottle tops or any plastic screw tops from tubes. Marbles, shells, buttons, beads, cotton reels, dried beans and peas, pearl barley and rice. Milk tops and metal foil pie containers, matchsticks, lollysticks, ice cream sticks, slats from date boxes, plum and peach stones, driftwood, bark or cork that you can pick up on the beaches, old wooden toy bricks, broom handles, even pieces from broken wooden and plastic toys. There are lots of other things. You will enjoy collecting them and finding out what kind of patterns they make.

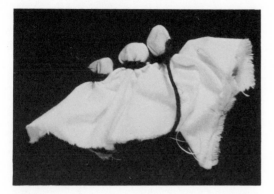

This shows how to do the binding. Tie the thread round the first object, bind it in properly then take the thread along and wrap it round the next object several times. There is no need to make a slip knot in between. When all the binding is finished make a slip knot round the last object. (See illustrations on pages 50 to 53.

STONES AND SMALL OBJECTS

Plan the arrangements of the objects in the cloth. If they are to be put in a straight line, make a crease in the cloth, and follow that. With a more complicated design put pencil dots to indicate where the objects are to be placed. Work from one side of the sample to the other or from the centre, outwards.

Vary the spacing and put objects together of different sizes.

Tie in some objects before the first dyeing and the rest before the second dyeing. Dye bands of colour on the cloth before tying in any of the objects.

Dye the background *only* in a different colour (see pages 137 and 138).

This shows a design made by binding small pebbles into velveteen.

A pattern made by tying trouser buttons and pearl barley in rows into the cloth. Lines of binding can be added in between the rows of objects to enrich the design.

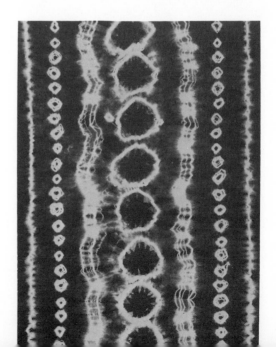

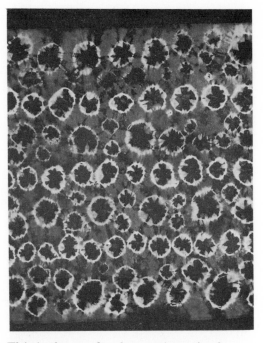

This is the result when various-sized stones are bound into the cloth. After dyeing the first colour the background was marbled by taking binding thread in between the stones. Then the sample was dyed a darker colour. This gives a lively tone and colour contrast.

Some plastic bottle tops were bound in the cloth to form a repeat pattern. The background in between was bound loosely. This gives a marbled texture as well as the design from the bottle tops.

Effect when a small piece of polythene is bound over each stone. In this case the binding was taken some way down below the stone to give a circle of texture.

Pattern effect when a metal milk top is placed under the cloth. Both are squeezed up together and bound with thread.

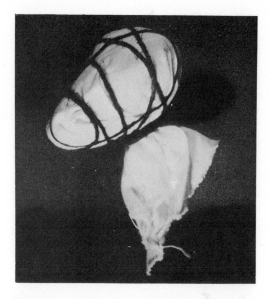

Wrap the cloth over a larger stone. Put binding underneath and over the stone in all directions.

This sample shows the effect when several larger stones were bound into the cloth as above, to form a repeat pattern.

To make a "neck" of binding. Tie some stones into the cloth. Make a second binding a little distance away from and below the first binding.

The design produced is a double resist ring.

Make a small fold in the cloth covering the stone. Add rubber rings or binding underneath.

Result after dyeing.

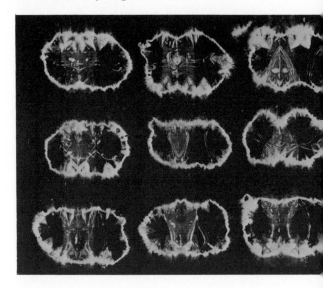

Dyed effect.

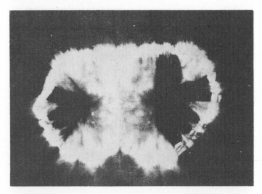

For this pattern make two tucks in the cloth. Pin in place but remove the pins before dyeing. Tie three larger stones under the tucks and put binding over and around the top.

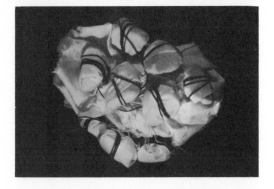

Make three tucks in the cloth. Pin them in place. Bind three small stones under each tuck. Take the binding over the top of the stones. This must be kept very taut or the binding will slip off during the dyeing. Remove pins.

Make flat tucks across some fine cloth. Pin in place. This gives three thicknesses of cloth. Bind three stones along each tuck. Remove pins. When dyed each stone gives a pattern of three resist rings.

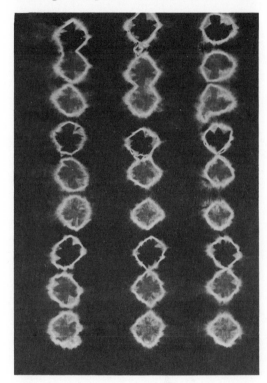

To prevent the binding slipping off larger stones during the dyeing, and also to make it possible to build up a richer area of texture, tie some very tiny stones in the cloth first of all. Then put these over a much larger stone. Use the small stones as "hitches" for the binding which can be twisted in all directions, enclosing the larger stone.

The effect when "hitches" are used for binding over a large stone.

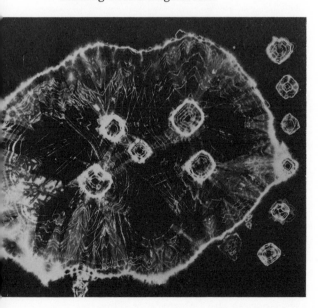

Make three upright tucks across the cloth. Bind stones in the upright parts. When dyed each stone gives a pattern of two resist rings. If the stones are tied in near the edge of the tuck the two resist rings mingle, to form a figure of eight.

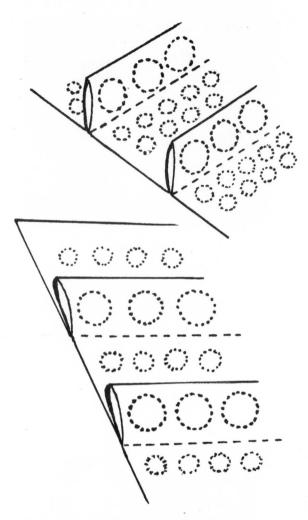

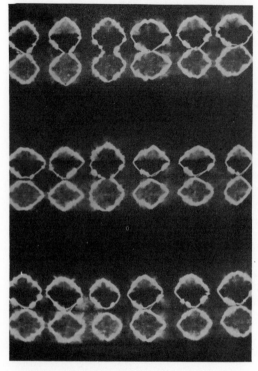

Stones or small objects can be bound in the tucks and also in the single cloth in between the tucks. The flat tucks (three thicknesses) and the upright tucks (two thicknesses) can be combined on one sample as a repeat pattern, alternate rows of each.

The pattern can be uniform, using similar objects, tied in at regular intervals over the fabric.

Flat tucks can be pinned in place over the whole sample, so that there are three thicknesses of cloth throughout. This gives a chance to tie the stones in at random, producing quite unexpected designs. Use thin cloth for this to allow the dye to penetrate.

The tucks can vary in size on one sample.

For a change, make tucks lengthways, or even diagonally, on the cloth.

BINDING OVER BASES

Binding will only produce a pattern where it grips the cloth covering the base tightly enough to keep out the dye. If the base has a hard flat surface the dye will seep between it and the binding in this area. To prevent this, tie wads of newspaper on the flat surfaces. This allows the binding thread to grip the cloth covering them sufficiently to produce a good resist. Round surfaces, although hard, a broom handle for instance, do not need padding.

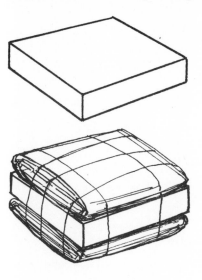

Foam rubber can be used to wrap round the flat surfaces instead of the newspaper. Hold it in place with a rubber ring or binding thread. For these methods the binding must be pulled very taut.

Put a quantity of milk tops or other small objects in a piece of cloth. Squeeze into a lump. Add binding underneath and over the lump in all directions. Several such lumps can be made at intervals over a length of cloth.

Effect after dyeing.

Tie two cotton reels (or similar) together, threaded on a piece of string. Drape the cloth over these and bind over each one. For a larger piece of cloth thread more cotton reels on the piece of string and bind the cloth over each one. Alternatively, the two cotton reels design can be repeated where required on the cloth.

The dyed pattern.

Effect after dyeing.

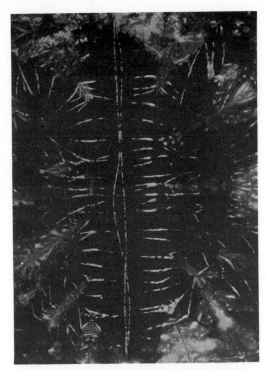

Look round for other suitable "bases" on which to drape and bind cloth.

Wrap the cloth over a circular piece of cork with a hole in the centre (as used for lobster pots or fishing nets). Bind with string around the outside and over in all directions.

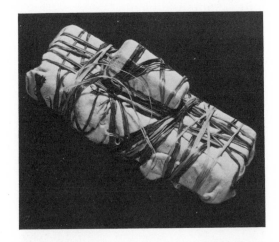

Tie a small piece of wood on top of a larger piece. Cover with cloth. Bind with raffia in all directions.

Dyed design.

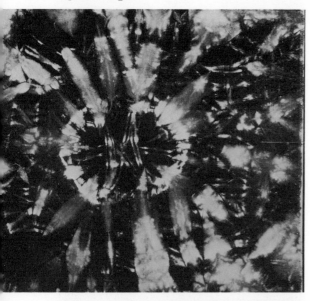

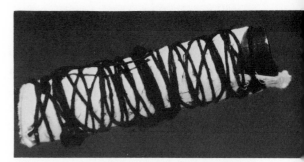

Fold cloth into four or six lengthways. Roll this tube of cloth diagonally round a piece of broom handle or a piece of cork, etc. Bind very firmly with string.

Result after one dyeing. Untie. Fold cloth again so that the less well dyed part comes to the outside. Roll this on the base and bind as before.

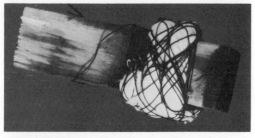

Gather cloth up to form a tube lengthways. Coil this round a piece of wood. Bind with thread or string.

Effect after dyeing.

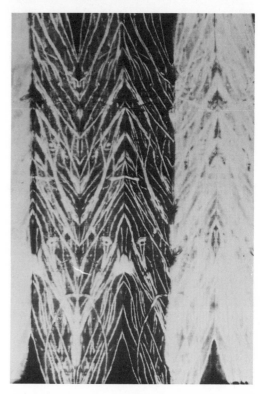

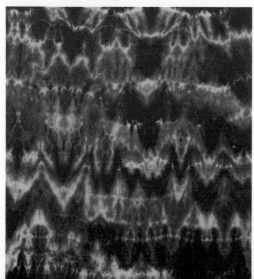

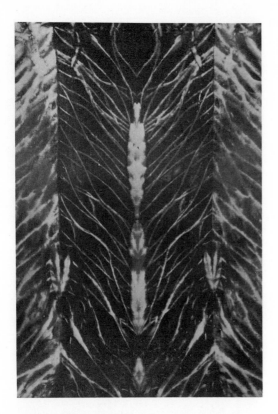

Make a tuck down the centre of a small piece of cloth then a tuck across it. Pin in place. Put this over two corks tied together or a piece of wood, etc. Bind very firmly with string.

Effect after dyeing.

Effect after folding the cloth into four and dyeing twice.

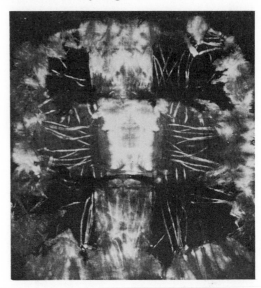

Dyed pattern.

Find a large, round, fluted plastic top. Fold a small piece of cloth in quarters. Place the centre of the cloth over the centre top of the plastic gadget. Turn each of the four folds down over the sides to make tucks, all falling in one direction. Add binding around it.

Find several plastic gadgets that stack closely within each other. Wrap the cloth over No 1. Push this inside No 2. Wrap more cloth over No 2. Push this into No 3, and so on. Add binding to tether them together securely.

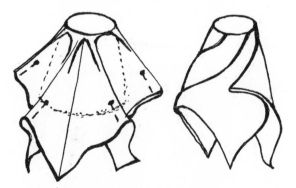

Result after one dyeing. Untie. Fold up
again as before but with the undyed
areas to the edges of the sample.
Sandwich between two sticks, add rubber
rings and dye a second colour.

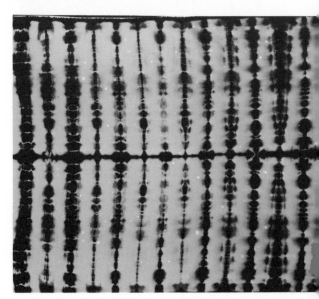

Effect after dyeing.

CLOTH SANDWICHED BETWEEN WOOD

For this method, two thin flat pieces of
wood similar in size are required, such as
lollysticks, ice cream sticks, slats from
old date boxes, plywood, etc.

Fold a small piece of cloth until it is just
slightly bigger than the two sticks. Sandwich the folded cloth between the two
sticks. Criss-cross several rubber rings
along the bundle.

Fold a larger piece of cloth and sandwich
it between two pieces of wood, in this
case two slats from a date box. Add
criss-cross binding with thread or string.

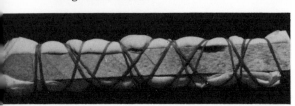

Dyed pattern.

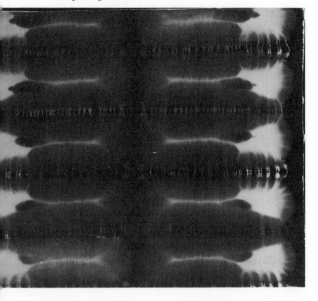

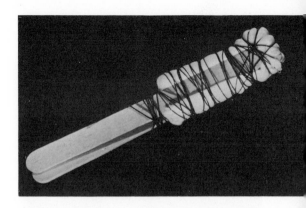

Fold a small piece of cloth into four lengthways and then across. Sandwich it at one end of two small sticks but let the cloth project at the top and sides. Add binding all around it.

Effect after one dyeing.

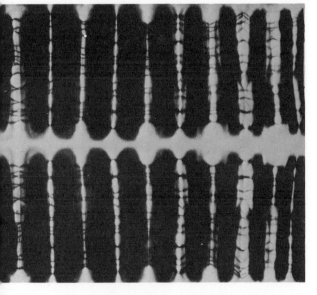

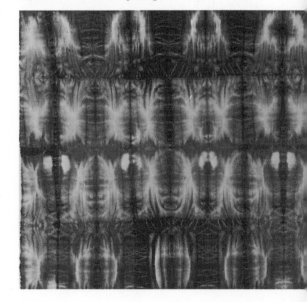

This is a bleached sample. Fold a piece of dyed or tie-dyed cloth and sandwich it between two date box slats as above. Add binding. Wet out, then dip in bleach until the colour changes or bleaches out. Rinse well. Rinse again after untying. Reactive dyes do not bleach easily so use cloth dyed in household or direct dyes.

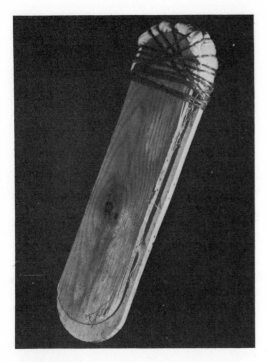

Fold a large piece of cloth and sandwich it between the ends of two date box slats. Add binding.

Result after dyeing.

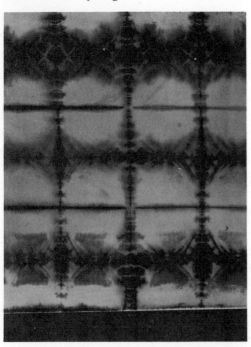

The cloth can be folded diagonally and in many different ways—before being put between two pieces of wood. When dyeing a second colour always untie your sample and re-arrange it so that the undyed parts come to the edge of the folds. Always wet out the sample before dyeing.

STRIPES MADE ON WOODEN SUPPORTS

Use matchsticks for a small narrow piece of cloth. Crease the cloth across into folds at regular intervals. Gather the first fold across to form a loop. Put a matchstick through it. Twist a rubber ring under it and around it. Repeat at each fold.

Use lollysticks or ice cream sticks for a medium piece of cloth in the same way as above. Make a binding with thread in place of the rubber ring. Take the binding diagonally over the top of the cloth on the lollystick, this makes a binding in the form of a cross.

Half the number of matchsticks or lollysticks can be put in for the first dyeing and the ones in between tied in before dyeing the second colour.

Stripes on wooden supports using longer lengths of cloth.

Make the bands much further apart on the cloth. Mark the folds of cloth with chalk or pencil accurately. Use thicker and larger pieces of wood to put inside the folds. Gather up the double cloth in your hands some way below the fold. Put on a rubber ring to make a tunnel of cloth. Place the wood inside and bind over it, in all directions with string—raffia, tape or strips of nylon stocking.

To get a broken, uneven stripe add corks, cotton reels, stones or any other small objects at intervals inside the fold of cloth. Put these on both sides of the wood. First tie them in the cloth and bind over them with a finer binding thread. Then bind in the wood so that the small objects project on it like knobs.

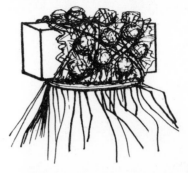

After the first dyeing you can make a line of binding between the bands. This will give a striped background to the pattern.

These bands of pattern can be made diagonally on the cloth. To do this, turn up one corner of the cloth to meet the opposite edge. Crease. This gives an angle of 45°. Crease or draw lines at intervals parallel with the first line.

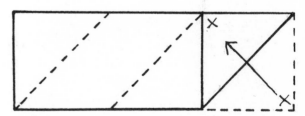

If you have some *very* fine cloth a chevron-shaped band of pattern is possible. Fold the cloth in half lengthways, then work on the double cloth as if making the diagonal bands of pattern. Fold a *square* of cloth in half across or diagonally. Insert a piece of wood in the fold, gather the cloth over it and add binding. Bind the ends of cloth before the first or second dyeing.

5 SAFETY-PIN METHOD

A SINGLE DIAMOND

Fold the cloth over double. Draw half the diamond against the fold. Weave a large safety-pin in and out along the pencil line. Close the pin.

Add binding to the small fan-like shape.

The diamond pattern when dyed.

Put enough binding under the pin to hold the gathered up cloth in place. Remove the pin.

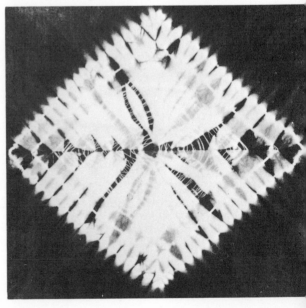

SEVERAL OVALS OR DIAMONDS

Draw half of each shape against the fold of cloth. Weave a safety-pin along the first shape.

Bind it and remove the pin. Repeat this for the next shape, using the same kind of binding or a different type.

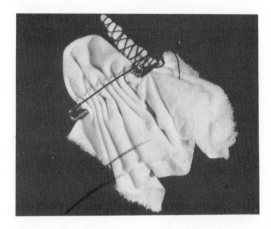

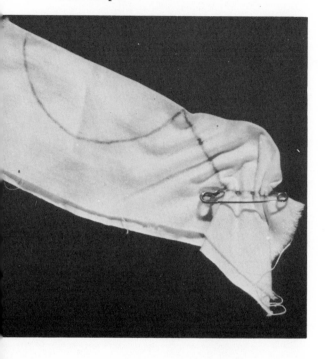

Any small symmetrical shape can be produced by this method. Ovals, diamonds, circles and petal shapes are perhaps the easiest to make. Several shapes can be grouped together. These can be repeated over a length of fine to medium cloth. The size of the shapes is limited to the amount of cloth you can squeeze on a safety-pin.

Dyed effect.

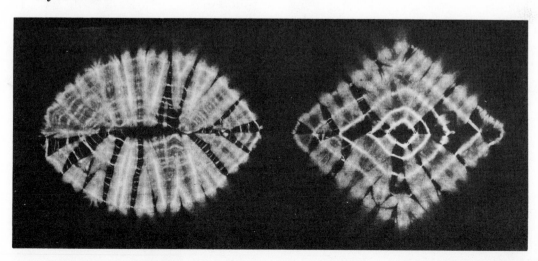

This shows an arrangement where one diamond is placed above the other—not alongside it as on the previous page. This would require two separate folds, one for each diamond.

These two small ovals placed side by side had a line of binding made *underneath* the two bound shapes. This enfolded them in a larger oval. Other shapes can be used in the same way.

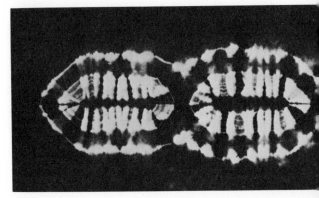

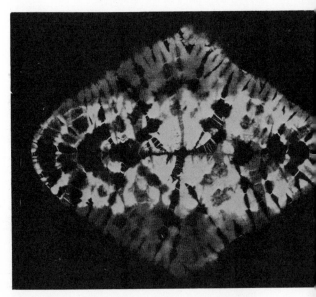

This design was dyed in two stages. The first layer was a pleated oval. After dyeing and untying, a pleated diamond was made on the same fold of cloth. This was dyed a second colour. Reactive dyes are best for this.

BANDS OF TEXTURE

Suitable for small samples. Use stainless
steel safety-pins as they are left on the
cloth while it is being dyed.

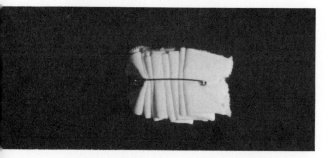

Fold a small piece of cloth into four
lengthways. Weave the pin in and out
along the middle of the folded cloth, as
if making large tacking stitches. Close
the pin. The cloth must be threaded on
to the pin in a very compact bundle. If it
is at all slack, thread a bead or several
buttons on the pin before closing it.
This pushes the cloth along the pin and
bunches it up close enough to produce a
good resist.

The dyed design.

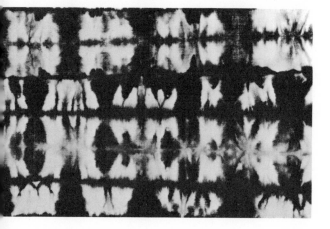

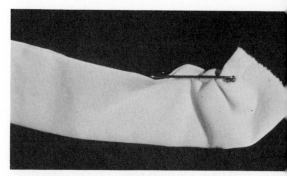

Fold the cloth into four. Weave a large
safety-pin over the edges as if oversewing.
As before the cloth must be packed
tightly on the safety-pin.

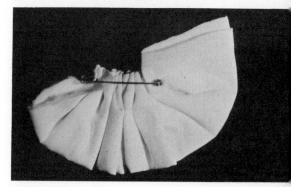

Add beads or buttons if there is any
spare room on the safety-pin.

Effect after dyeing.

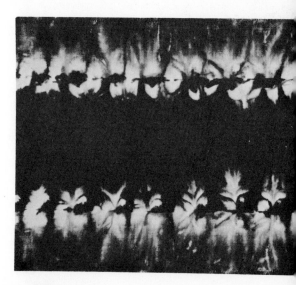

These methods can be adapted for longer
lengths of cloth. Use several safety-pins
along each fold. This will mean leaving
small gaps in between the safety-pins,
making, in effect, a regular repeat unit.

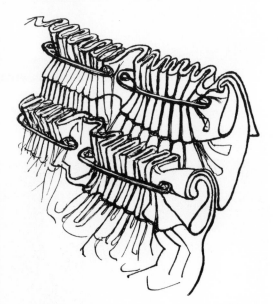
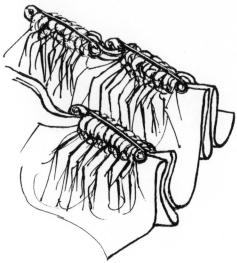

6
PLEATING

Suitable for all kinds of cloth. This method makes splendid panels for wall hangings, cushion covers, etc. The dyed shapes can be repeated over several yards of cloth to make up into curtains, bedspreads, tablecloths, etc. After the first dyeing add to or change the bindings before dyeing the second or third colour. The sample can be untied and tied up again, before the second or third dyeing. The tips of the shapes or the lower edges can be dyed a further or different colour from the main sample.

A LARGE CIRCLE

Fold the cloth over double. Mark the centre of the circle O on the fold. Around this, draw several semi-circles, graduating in size, and some distance apart. Cut several pieces of string about 12 ins long.

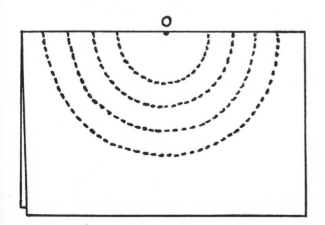

Begin with the smallest semi-circle and work with both hands. "Nibble" little pleats of cloth along the outline of the semi-circle from the folded edge downwards, until both hands meet in the centre. Transfer all the pleats to the left hand. Pick up a piece of string and make a binding on the bunched up outline. Tie the string into a knot. Pleat up each of the semi-circles in turn and put a binding round each one.

It may be easier to do the pleating while the sample is flat on the table. For a

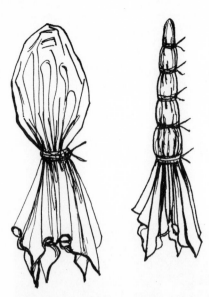

medium-sized circle the outside semi-
circle, only, need be drawn and "nibbled"
into pleats. Add binding to the fan-like
shape. After that pull the centre point
up and add bindings where required.

OVALS AND DIAMONDS

Oval and diamond shapes can be pleated
in the same way. Draw half the shape
against the fold of cloth. After tying up
the circle, oval or diamond, bind up the
corners and ends of the rectangle of cloth
to fit in with the pattern.

For a length of several yards, plan your
pattern carefully. Decide whether one
large shape or several smaller ones are to
be made on each fold, across or down
the cloth. Mark the centre point of each
shape on the folded cloth. Pleat along
the pencil outlines as described above.
Add the required amount of binding.

7 FOLDING & TYING SQUARES OF CLOTH

Any reasonable size. Fine fabric is easiest to work with, in the beginning, as the dye penetrates well, giving a balanced design. Handkerchiefs, old or new, of all sizes are particularly useful for these methods.

Almost any way of folding a square of cloth and adding rubber rings or binding gives an interesting pattern. It is a good plan to experiment with paper first to find different ways of folding squares. When a thicker cloth is used, or, if a design is patchy after the first dyeing, refold it, bringing the part that needs more dye to the outside before dyeing the next colour. A larger sample sometimes needs three dyeings to make a satisfying design.

The following diagrams analyse some simple methods of obtaining standard patterns on squares of cloth. Dotted lines show direction of the lines of binding.

Fold the square into quarters (1 and 6). Now gather, pleat (2) or roll (3) the sample in preparation for the lines of binding (4 and 5). Where the binding runs horizontally below the centre point 0 (1), the design produced will be like 7. If only part of the sample is bound (5) the design will appear as 8 whether pleated or rolled. Where the lines of binding run vertically (6) the result will be as 9 whether pleated or rolled.

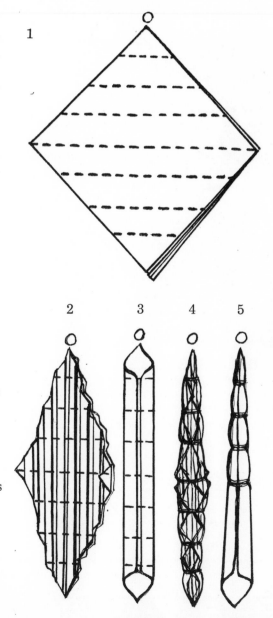

1

2   3   4   5

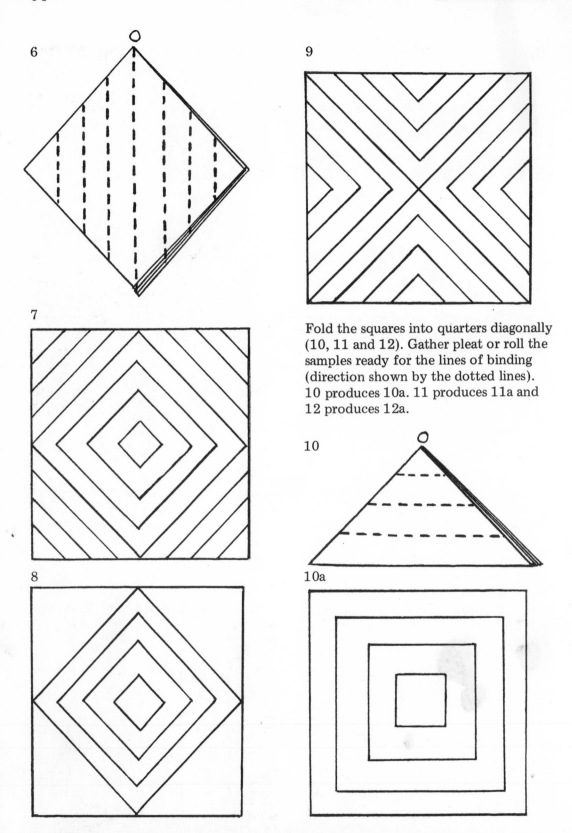

Fold the squares into quarters diagonally (10, 11 and 12). Gather pleat or roll the samples ready for the lines of binding (direction shown by the dotted lines). 10 produces 10a. 11 produces 11a and 12 produces 12a.

11

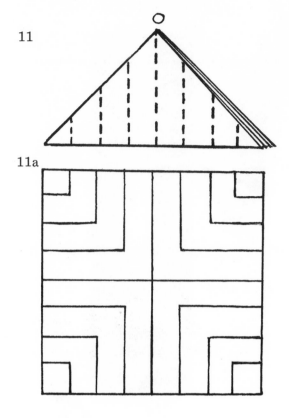

11a

12

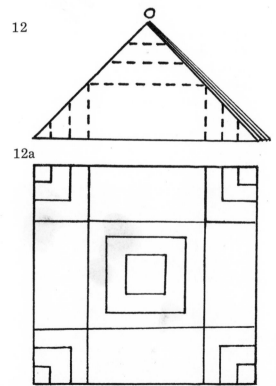

12a

An easy method for a first experiment. Fold a small square of cloth into quarters. Add binding (without tying knots) below the centre point for some way. Make a binding down from the opposite corner. Fasten off the binding with rubber rings. After the first dyeing, untie. Rearrange the cloth and tie up again as before.

Design after two dyeings.

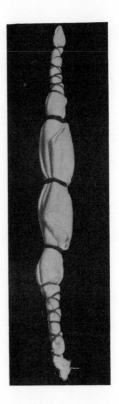

This is folded as on previous page but line bindings were made instead of criss-cross binding.

Fold a square of fine cloth into quarters, then over in half to form a triangle. Pleat the central point over towards the fold, to make a tube-like bundle. Add rubber rings or binding. Dye two colours, undoing the sample in between. Dye the ends another colour, one that is brighter or darker than the rest of the sample.

Finished effect.

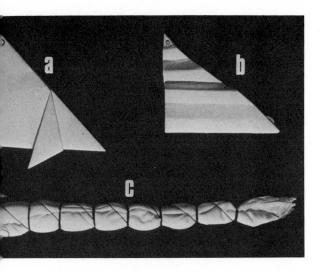

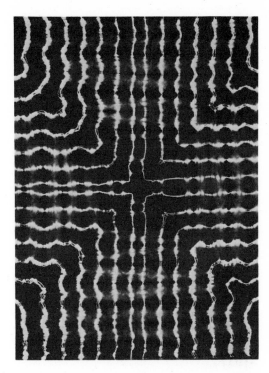

A. Fold a square of cloth into quarters, then across into a triangle.

B. Pleat the sample across from the centre point O to the outside edge.

C. Make line bindings at intervals.

Dyed design.

This is a one-yard square scarf of Viyella fabric, tied up as in diagrams 11 and 11*a* and dyed dry to allow the dye to penetrate. The edges are fringed.

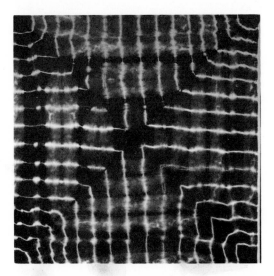

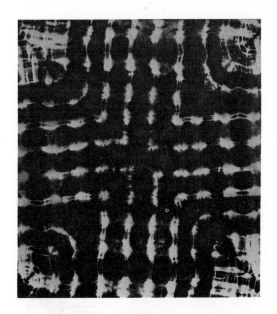

Tied up as above. Bands of criss-cross binding used.

Tied up as on previous page. The cloth had a previously tie-dyed background pattern.

Fold a square in half diagonally. Pleat the corners down to the fold to form the sample into a tube. Make line bindings on one side of the centre and bands of criss-cross binding on the other half. This sample was dyed three times, undone and re-tied for each dyeing. The bindings

were matched up with the previous ones, that is, they were made on the resist areas. Reactive dyes were used.

Fold a square of fine cloth into quarters diagonally. Make line bindings at each of the three corners. Pleat the corners so that the lines of binding follow the warp and weft of the sample. To make the direction more accurate these lines can be drawn in pencil before pleating up the cloth, or a tacking stitch made along each outside line, and drawn up before putting on the binding. Dye one or more colours. (See diagrams 12 and 12*a* on page 95.)

Fold the four corners of a square over to meet at the centre. This forms a smaller square sample. Pin the corners in place. Fold this smaller square into quarters. Remove the pins. Put a small binding to hold the corners in place in the centre. Make a binding at the opposite corner. Add criss-cross binding for some distance down at the two remaining corners. Dye two or more colours.

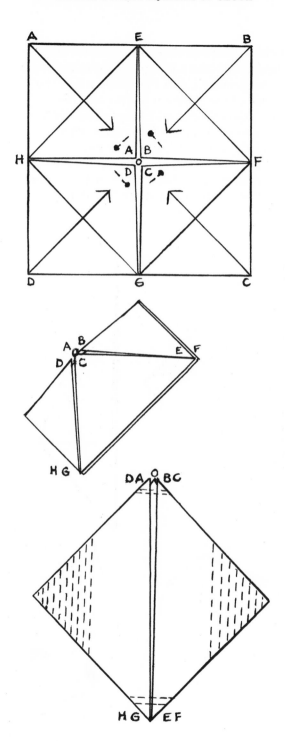

The dyed result.

Fold as above. Add more binding at the centre point and the opposite corners and less at the other two corners. Dye two colours.

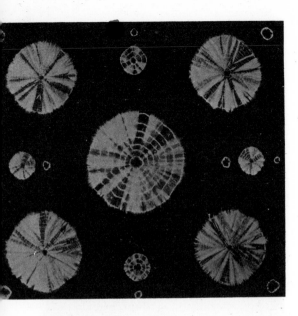

Fold a square of cloth into quarters and then across into a triangle. Fold in half again to make a dart-like shape where the centre of the square is the point at the top. Fold this dart-like shape, diagonally at intervals from top to bottom. This makes a flattened spiral tube. Pin in place. Add lines of binding where each diagonal turn has been made. A little open binding can be made at the top and bottom of the sample.

This is an arrangement of circles and spots on a square of cloth.

A SQUARE WITH A STAR DESIGN

Small to medium-sized samples using fine cloth are most suitable.

1. Folding method

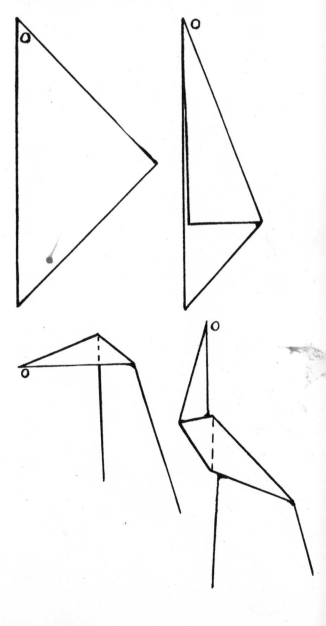

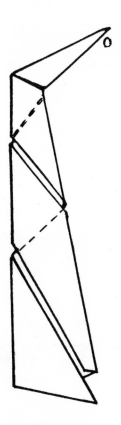

Dyed star design.

2. Rolling method

Beginning at the top, roll the dart-like sample spirally round a pencil or something similar. Put on several rubber rings to hold it in place. Take the pencil out. Add bindings as in folding method above.

3. Sewing and binding method

Draw zig-zig lines on the dart-shaped sample from top to bottom. Thread a needle with double thread. Make a large knot and then tack along the pencil lines. Take the stitches over the folded edges of cloth at each side. Tighten up the thread by pulling, if it is a small fine sample. Add bindings along each line of sewing. Put criss-cross bindings at the top and bottom if required.

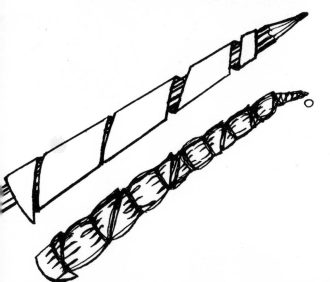

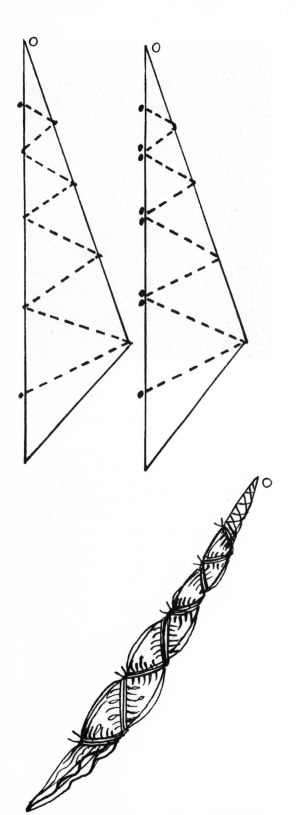

On a larger sample cut the threads at one side. At each cut, knot both ends of thread. Pull up the threads and tie them as shown. Add bindings along each line of sewing. Wet out small samples before dyeing. Large ones, dye dry. If the pattern is patchy, refold the sample, bringing the undyed areas to the outside. Repeat the whole process before dyeing the next colour.

Effect when the design is made by sewing.

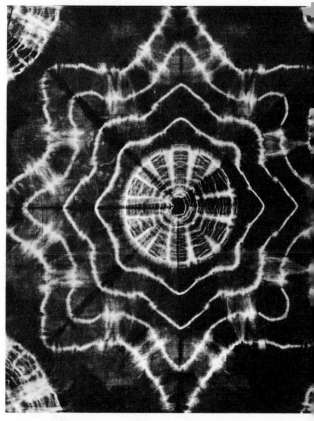

8
ROLLING METHODS

THE SNAKE PATTERN

This name has been given because the pattern looks very much like "snakeskin". It is a particularly attractive method for scarves, stoles or narrow strips of cloth. Fine to medium-grained cloth is best. Thick cloth is not suitable. You will require a piece of rope slightly longer than your sample.

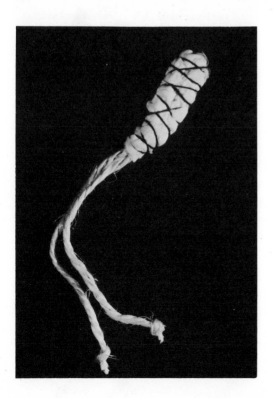

Straight rolling on rope.

Place the rope at one side of a piece of single cloth. Roll the rope, covered with the cloth over to the opposite side. There is now a tube of cloth. Fold this over in half. Hold the ends of rope while pushing the cloth away and up towards the centre. Bunch it up as far as it will go. Tie the two ends of rope together into a knot. This keeps the cloth from slipping down. Bind over the gathered cloth. Dye dry or wet. Rinse and untie.

Repeat the whole process but this time begin by placing the rope against the other side. This was on the outside for the first dyeing. In the second dyeing the cloth that was inside before, should now be on the outside.

There are very many ways of folding and rolling the cloth. Each one produces bands of pattern in different places on the sample.

Try out any of the diagrams on pages 46 and 47.

After experimenting with this method you will realise that a stronger band of pattern is made on the cloth which is on the outside of the roll.

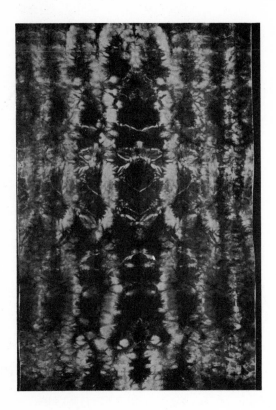

A longer sample of fine cloth rolled and
bound as above but dyed dry to allow
better penetration.

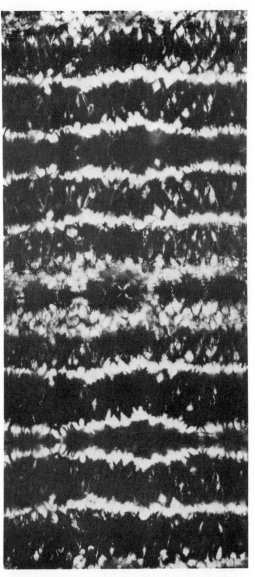

This shows the pattern achieved when a
length of fine cloth is folded into four
across before rolling it on the rope. Dyed
dry.

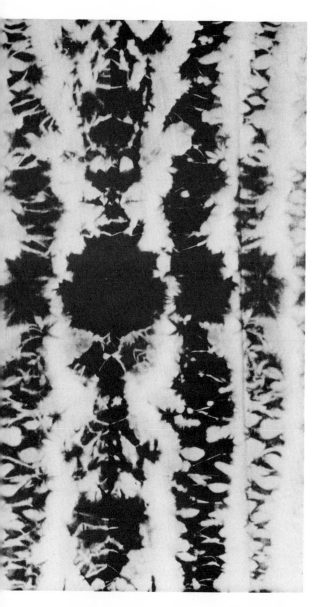

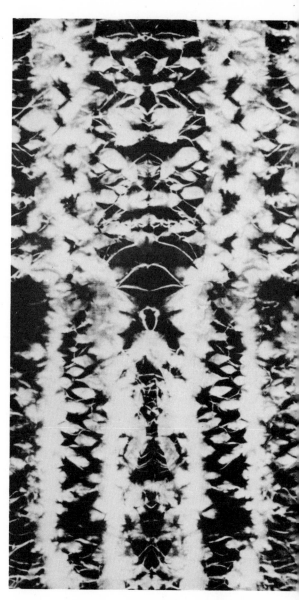

This sample shows the effect after one dyeing when the cloth is folded in half lengthways. It is then rolled from the outer edges across to the fold (see page 47).

Effect after the second dyeing. The sample is rolled in the opposite direction before being dyed.

Pattern after one dyeing. Untie the sample. Roll up the cloth as before, beginning at the *adjacent* corner.

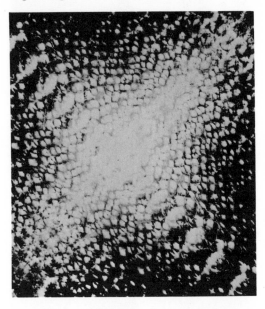

Right: place the rope at one corner of the sample. Roll it in the cloth diagonally across to the opposite corner (p. 48). Fold it in the centre. Push the cloth on the rope up to the centre. Tie the two ends of rope together.

Left: add binding.

This is how it looks after the second dyeing.

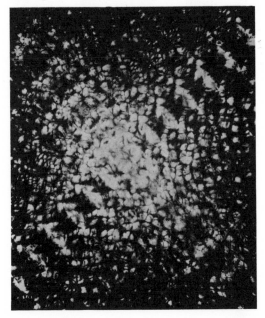

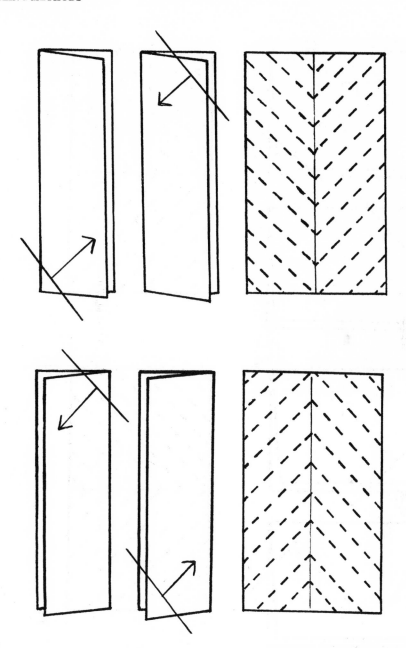

Diagonal rolling on cloth folded in half lengthwise.

If a sample is folded before rolling, when tying it up for the second colour, turn the sample over from back to front and roll from the opposite corner.

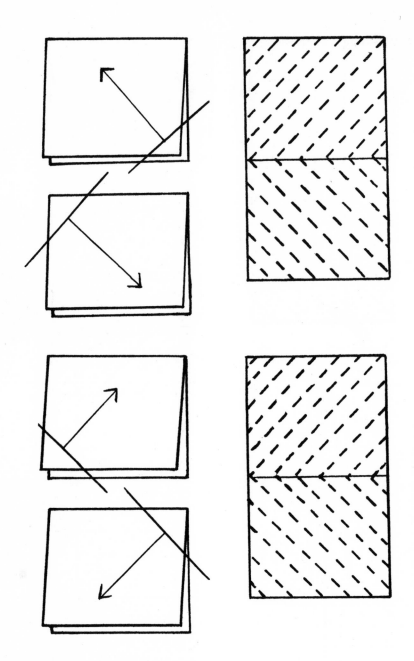

Diagonal rolling on cloth folded in half
across.

Diagonal rolling on folded cloth

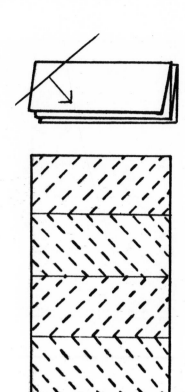

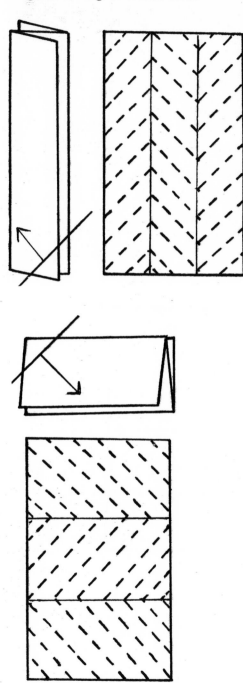

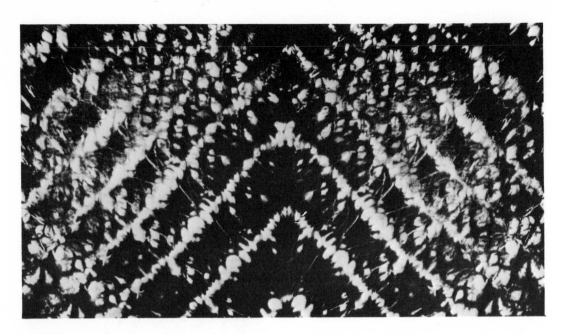

For this pattern the cloth is folded in half across. It is then rolled diagonally from one corner across to the opposite corner.

Rolling without rope

Use fine cloth and fine binding thread. Small to medium pieces of cloth.

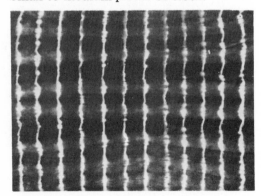

Place the cloth on a flat surface. To begin with use a fine knitting needle (one without a knob) on which to roll the cloth. Place it along the side of the cloth nearest to you. Roll the cloth on the knitting needle across to the opposite side. Remove the knitting needle. Make line bindings or narrow criss-cross bands along the roll (pp. 54, 66, 67). Dye wet or dry. Rinse and untie. Re-roll the cloth as before, placing the knitting needle against the well-dyed side that was on the outside of the roll. This should be inside this time. Bind as before. Dye again, in the same or a different colour.

Having done this easy sample it is possible to experiment with this method at great lengths. There are many fascinating variations (see page 157).

1 Make a tuck in the cloth and roll diagonally.

2 Make a diagonal fold in the cloth and roll.

Dyed effect.

3 Turn the corners over at an angle.

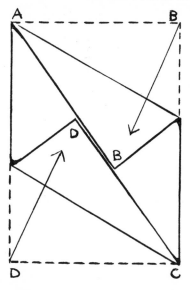

Dyed effect.

4 Vary the spacing of the bindings, graduating from very close ones to ones further apart.

5 Add extra bindings in between the first bindings before dyeing the second colour.

6 Dye the ends different colours.

7 Roll the cloth diagonally either single or folded.

All these methods of rolling are shown on page 157.

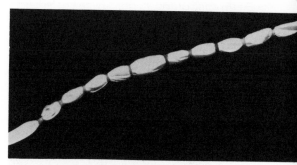

The sample shows the use of small rubber rings in place of the line or narrow bindings generally made. This means that beginners can use these methods even if the binding is too difficult. Fold a square of cloth in half diagonally. Roll the points across to the folded edge. Put small rubber rings on the roll at intervals.

Pattern of dyed diagonal stripes.

A CHEVRON PATTERN

This is suitable for a tie or scarf, or panels for a skirt or dress.
Fold the cloth in half lengthways. Roll this double narrow strip of cloth diagonally. It may be easier to roll it on a piece of string or a roll of polythene. Begin the rolling at the lower cut edge corners and work upwards. The folded edge should be on the outside of the roll. Make line bindings along the roll. Wet out and dye. Rinse and untie. You will find there is now a chevron pattern down the centre of the sample.

If you need to dye it again so that the outside edges have a more definite pattern:

1. For chevrons going in the *same* direction as before, but with the dyed areas concentrated at the two sides, fold the sample and roll up as before but begin at the *opposite* end and with the *folded* edge corner, this time. Bind as before, in the same resist lines if possible. Dye a second colour.

2. For chevrons going in the *opposite* direction and with the dyed areas concentrated at the two sides, fold the sample and roll up as before but this time begin at the same end as the first dyeing and work from the folded edge corner. This brings the cut edges to the outside of the roll of cloth. Bind as required and dye the second colour. To even out the heavily-dyed areas still more, turn the sample over back to front before rolling as Methods 1 or 2 for the second colour. Dye dry if more penetration is needed.

To make a double chevron or zig-zag pattern, fold the narrow strip of cloth into four lengthways before rolling.

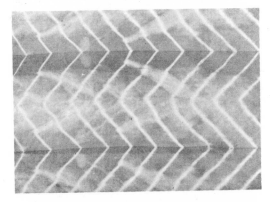

Folding it into six will give three
chevrons and into eight will give four
chevrons.

It is possible to use these methods for
larger and longer pieces of cloth. If so,
leave more space between each binding
and dye dry.

9

PIN-PIVOT METHOD

This method is used mainly for square or rectangular panels of fine to medium thickness fabric.

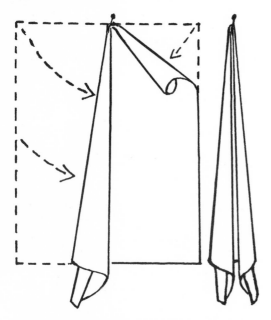

Place the cloth flat on a thick wad of newspaper, on a carpet or some other surface that will hold a pin. Push the pin through the centre point at the top of the rectangle and into the newspaper or carpet underneath. The pin must tether the cloth firmly. Pulling against the pin, using it as a pivot, *roll* or *pleat* the cloth on either side of it down to the middle of the sample. Pin in place, put on a rubber ring or a loose binding. Lift up the sample, take out the pivot pin. Stretch the roll of cloth. Make line

bindings from the point down to the lower edge.

The bindings can be made closer together on the thin part of the roll—that is, at the top—and wider apart towards the bottom where the sample is bulkier. This applies to all samples where rolling and the pin pivot method are used.

SEMI-CIRCLES

This is the design produced, a half concentric circle or concentric radiating lines.

All rolled and pin pivot methods can be partially bound for the first colour and more binding added for the second colour.

Also, bindings can be made in between the existing ones, before dyeing the second colour.

This same method gives different patterns according to how the cloth is folded and where the pin is placed. The following are some of the possibilities:

CIRCLES ROLLED ON DOUBLE CLOTH

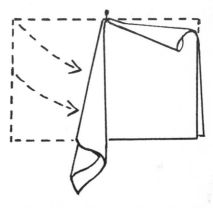

Fold the sample in half across. Place the pin at the centre point just below the fold. *Never* put the pin on the edge of the fold or a hole may be torn right in the middle of your sample. Put the pin about $\frac{1}{8}$-$\frac{1}{4}$ inch down from the fold. Begin rolling on either side of the pin. Add bindings and dye one or two colours.

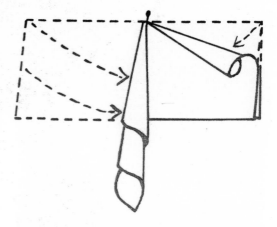

TWO SEMI-CIRCLES BACK TO BACK

When dyeing a rectangle of cloth, it can be folded in half lengthways. The pin for pivoting can be placed in the centre or off-centre on either the folded edge or the cut edges.

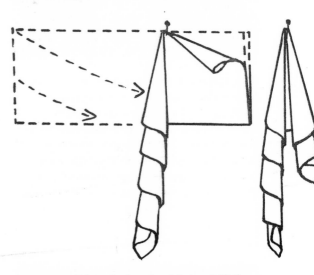

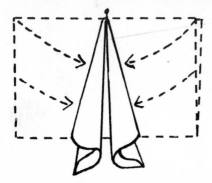

If the pin is placed at the centre of the *cut* edges instead of on the fold as the previous sample, the result will be two concentric semi-circles back to back.

A very striking design is obtained if the pin is placed on the folded edge for the first dyeing to give a circle. After untying place the pin on the cut edges and bind to give two semi-circles. Use contrasting coloured dyes.

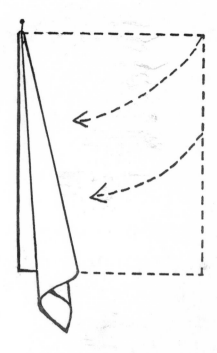

Another attractive variation of this method, using a square of cloth.
Fold the square in half diagonally. Turn the sample so that the points are at the top. Put a pin in the double cloth just below the tip of the points A and C (these are right-angled corners). Roll the double edges B and D on either side of the pin down towards the centre of the fold O (see diagram 13 on page 24). Add bindings. The sample above shows the result after two dyeings.

Try combinations of these methods on a sample.

Small to medium-sized samples are best for the following, preferably rectangles, not squares.

Stick the pin on one corner of a single piece of cloth. Roll the short side nearest the pin across and over to the longer side at right angles to it. Lift up the sample, remove the pin. Give the roll a pull. Add line bindings right along it, the design is more effective if the bindings are made close together at the tip and further apart towards the lower edge. Dye the first colour.

On this sample lines of bindings were added in between the previous ones before dyeing the second colour.

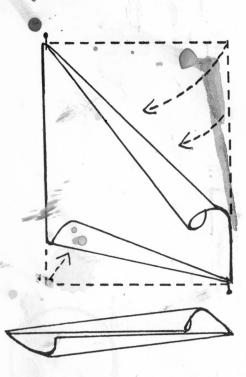

Variations on the last two methods can
be made by folding the cloth across,
lengthways or, if very fine cloth, into
quarters.

Place a rectangle of cloth flat on the
carpet or on newspaper. Stick one pin
in the top corner and another in the
lower corner diagonally opposite it. Roll
the top short side down as far as the
imaginary diagonal line between the two
pins. Roll the bottom short side up
until the two rolls meet. There are now
two rolls running diagonally across the
cloth, meeting in the centre. Put a loose
binding on, or rubber rings. Lift the
sample up, give it a stretch. Add line
bindings—close together at each end and
further apart in the middle.

The sample shows the design after two
dyeings.

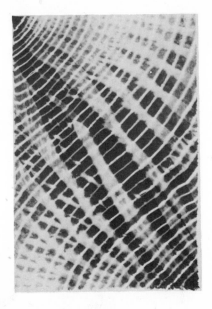

10 SIMPLE SEWING METHODS

All kinds of cloth.

Thread should be very strong and not too bulky. Thick thread leaves holes in the cloth. Button-hole thread, fine linen thread or strong thread as used by tailors, all used double, give good results.

The advantage of using double, medium thickness thread is that it slips through the cloth smoothly, and, being double does not become unthreaded during use. Use crewel needles 3-7 for your sewing. The most important thing in the sewing method is to make a large knot when beginning the sewing and to fasten off securely. *Whenever* you cut a thread on a sample, *wherever* it is, always make a knot at the end.

To outline any shape drawn on the cloth:

Make one row of running or tacking stitches approx. ¼-½ inch in size on the line. Make a row on either side of the first row. This gives three rows of stitches to help make a good resist. If one line breaks when you pull up the thread then you still have two other lines of sewing. After you have finished all the sewing, pull up the threads and tie the ends together. The cloth must be bunched up really tightly on the sewing thread or the dye will soak through. Add a little binding if you wish. To fasten off when there is only one end, all you have to do is thread a second needle with a small amount of double thread. Make a knot at the end. Slip this small piece in beside the odd end. You can now tie these two ends together.

ALL-OVER TEXTURE

Suitable for small or large samples, most kinds of fabric.

Fold cloth, which in this case is
velveteen, in half lengthways. Make a
large knot in a long length of double
thread. Make rows of large tacking
stitches across from side to side of the
double cloth from one end of the sample
to the other. Pull the thread up tightly.
It may be necessary to cut it at the
selvedge edges and to tie the ends of two
rows together. Add a little binding here
and there if it appears too loose. Dye the
first colour. Wet your sewn samples to
help get a better resist. Add some bands
of binding before dyeing the second
colour.

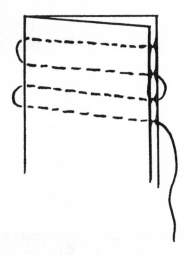

Lines of sewing can be made diagonally
on single cloth. On double cloth these
would produce a chevron-shaped pattern.

For the first experiments in sewing, wet
out the sample before dyeing.

A BAND OF TEXTURE

Suitable for most kinds of cloth.

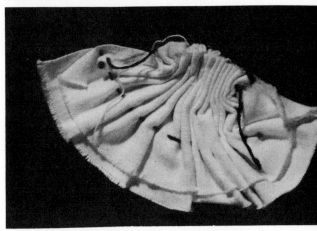

Make a fold along the cloth and run a
line of tacking stitches just below it.
Several rows of stitches make a more
effective pattern. Pull up the threads
tightly and fasten off securely.

Result after dyeing.

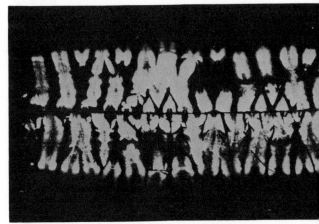

These bands of texture can be repeated
on tucks made across or down a length
of cloth. Before dyeing a second colour
extra lines of sewing can be made, or
binding over certain areas can be added.
Some lines of sewing can be left loose
during the first dyeing. These can be
pulled up before dyeing the second
colour. Flat tucks on the cloth can

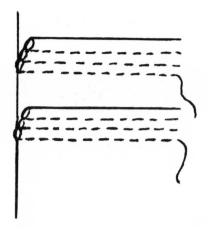

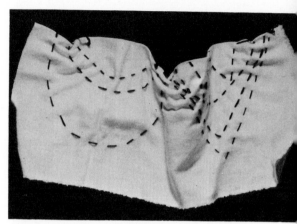

SYMMETRICAL DRAWN SHAPES

Large and small samples of all kinds of cloth.

have the lines of sewing across them at right angles. Another variation is to make diagonal lines of sewing across flat tucks made on the cloth (giving three thicknesses). For the flat tuck methods use only fine cloth.

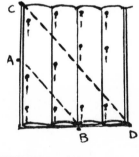

Fold the cloth over double. Draw half the required shape against the fold. With double thread tack along the pencil line. Make a second or third row to reinforce the first row. If more than one shape is planned complete all the sewing on the sample before tightening the threads. Fasten off.

Dyed design.

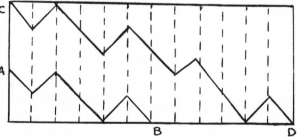

This gives a dyed design of zig-zig lines as shown above.

Binding can be added before the first or any subsequent dyeing.

Effect after dyeing. The sample was wetted out before dyeing.

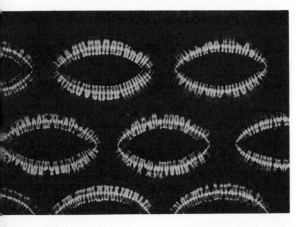

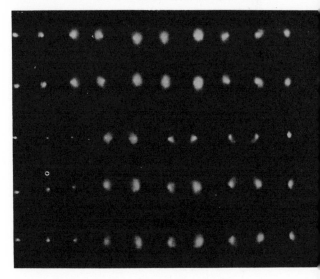

This pattern shows sewn ovals repeated over a length of cloth. Dyed two colours.

RUNNING STITCHES ON TUCKS

Straight sewing.

Cloth was folded into eight lengthways before being sewn as above.

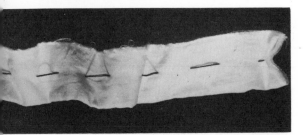

Fold a small piece of cloth into six or eight or until the sample is about 1½-2 ins wide. With double thread make a row of large tacking stitches 1-1½ ins long down the middle of the folded sample. Pull the thread up tightly and fasten off.

This forms the sample into a compact folded bundle like that shown on top of page 89.

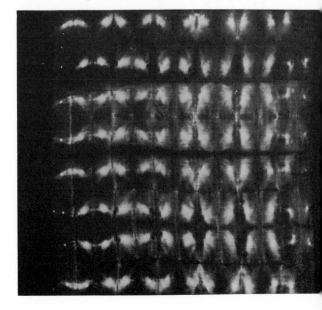

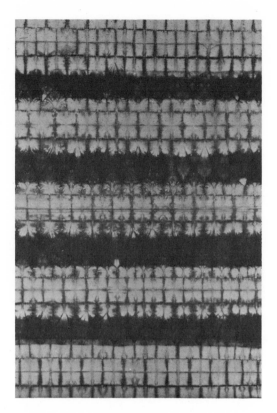

Work exactly as above but make *two* identical, parallel rows of tacking stitches along the folded cloth.

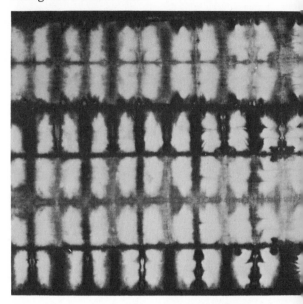

This sample shows how to repeat this method to make a pattern over a larger piece of cloth. Tucks are made across the cloth at intervals and pinned in place. Each tuck is turned over a second time as if making a hem. This gives five thicknesses of cloth. Each tuck has a row of tacking stitches along it.

Make single tucks (of three thicknesses of cloth) over the whole sample. Pin in place but remove the pins before dyeing. Make two identical, parallel rows of tacking stitches with double thread, along each tuck. Pull up the threads and fasten off. Wet out before dyeing.

Pull up the sewing threads tightly. Wet out and dye.

Dyed result.

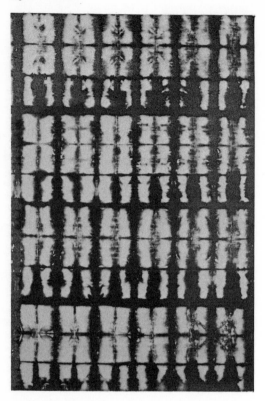

ZIG-ZAG STITCHING ON TUCKS

Fold a small piece of cloth into a tube
1½-2 ins wide. With double thread sew
large stitches in a zig-zag direction along
the cloth. Tighten the thread to form the
sample into a compact folded bundle (see
page 89). Dyed effect top left corner of
photo.

Use more and smaller stitches for the
zig-zag sewing. Always sew a regular
sequence of stitches on each row. This
means, each slope should have one stitch
throughout, as shown. Or, each slope
can have two or more stitches, but they
should all be alike.

Various samples showing effects when
more stitches make up the zig-zag lines
of sewing.

This method can also be used for longer
lengths of cloth. Form the sample into
tucks down or across and make a row of
zig-zag stitches on each one in turn. Pull
up sewing threads. Binding can be added
to the drawn-up triangular shapes.

OVERSEWING

All kinds of cloth, any size.

Thread a needle with double thread and
make a large knot. Sew over and over a
fold of cloth from one end to the other.

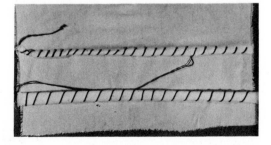

With a long row, after sewing a little way
pull the thread slightly so that the cloth

already sewn begins to curl round the thread. This helps to make the final pulling up easier. When all the sewing is done hold each row in your left hand and gradually pull the sewing thread taut. This bunches up the cloth. It should be so compact that the cloth coils over and completely covers the sewing thread. It now looks like a piece of cord. This method gives a line of texture.

For a wider band, roll the folded edge down some way like a hem. Sew over this roll but use bigger stitches. Begin to pull up the thread when you have sewn a little way. Tighten the thread finally when the row of sewing is finished. Fasten off securely (see p. 119, right column). The lines or bands of texture can be made across, down or diagonally across the cloth, and repeated at intervals.

Effects of bands of oversewing.

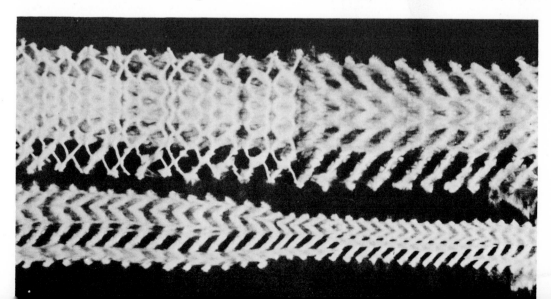

**A shape drawn on the cloth and
oversewn**

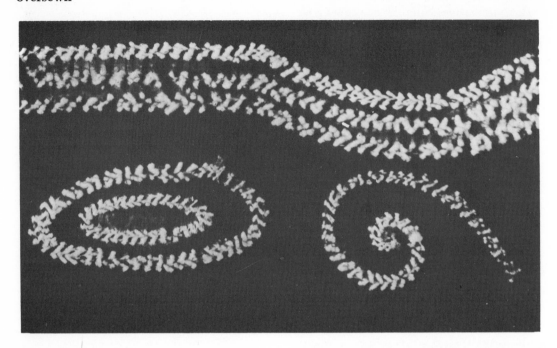

Any line or shape drawn freely on the
sample can be oversewn. Use double
thread. Keep the stitches moving in a
forward direction or the cloth will get
"jammed" when you try to tighten the
thread. Complete all the sewing on the
sample before fastening off. If you have
a sample with a long line of sewing it
may be difficult to tighten up in one go.
Cut the thread at given spots and pull up
small areas at a time. Fasten off each one
separately.

Wet these samples out before dyeing.

To begin with, try simple shapes. Add
binding after pulling up the thread, to
help the resist pattern. Some small stones
can be tied inside the shapes to add
interest to the design.

All your work will be in vain if the
sewing threads are not tightened enough
or the fastening-off is slack. If there are
many lines of sewing on a small design it
is sometimes difficult to tell whether
they have all been pulled up. One way of
checking up on this is to cut off the
knots that were made to begin and end
the line of sewing, after you have
tightened each thread and fastened off.
If you run your finger over the sample
and find a loose knot you will know
that one has escaped. You can then pick
up the knot, pull the thread and fasten
off.

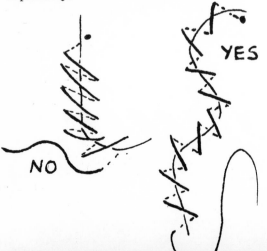

YES

NO

BUTTONS SEWN INTO THE CLOTH

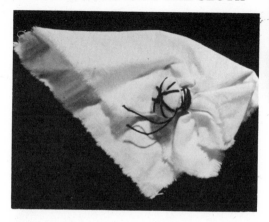

This sample had buttons with fluted edges sewn and bound into the cloth. The stitches were taken over the edge of the buttons.

Previously dyed thread can be used for sewing and binding the buttons.

Sew a button on to the back of the fabric so that the convex side is nearest the cloth. Arrange the stitches to form a design on the front face of the cloth. Sew the buttons in some sort of order or as part of a pattern. Turn the sample over and, on the right side, add binding under each button.

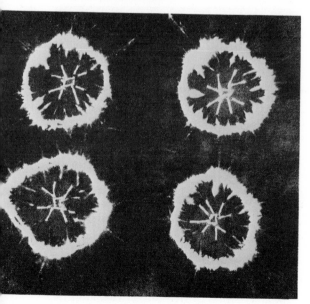

Effect when four trouser buttons are bound and sewn into the cloth.

11 DRAWN THREAD DESIGNS

Use small to medium samples of coarse-grained cloth. Linen or hessian, where the fibres are strong enough to pull loose without breaking are best. Linen is ideal as it takes the dyes so well.

Dye a sample with a simple pattern or shape in very strong colours. It must have a very definite white resist area. Pull certain threads out about ½-¾ inch from the edge on one, two or all sides of the sample. This gives a "shot" effect to the design. Do not pull too many of the threads or the result will become just a muddled mess. Choose carefully which threads to move. Try to make the "shot" pattern echo or reinforce the main design, not destroy it.

This is an example of a linen sample dyed with a definite resist pattern. The chosen threads are "moved" by pulling them about ¾-1 inch on one side only of the sample.

Here is a linen sample with a simple bold motif with a marked white resist. Draw the chosen threads about ¾ inch on two sides of the sample.

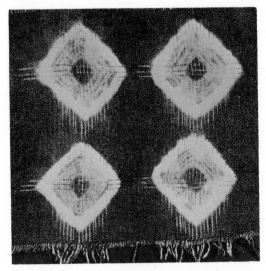

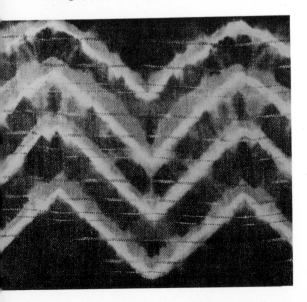

Threads can be drawn out of the sample completely, before it is tied up. This gives a lacy effect. After dyeing, other threads can still be drawn out on any side to give the "shot" effect.

11 & 12 Panels of small squares of cloth folded, bound and dyed individually and mounted on a tie-dyed background.

13 Panel of two handkerchiefs on tie-dyed background.

14 Velvet hanging sewn and bunched up by binding.

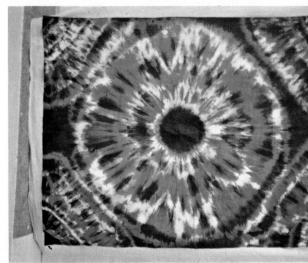

16 Red and blue panel: centre and four
outside corners knotted and dyed.

Here the linen had some threads drawn out completely before it was dyed. The resist stripes are made in between the drawn threads. Certain threads are then moved about 1½ inches on one side only.

This is a linen sample with a simple tie-dyed stripe pattern. After dyeing, draw two or three threads right out of the sample at intervals. Weave coloured embroidery threads in their place. Move other threads down about 1 inch to give

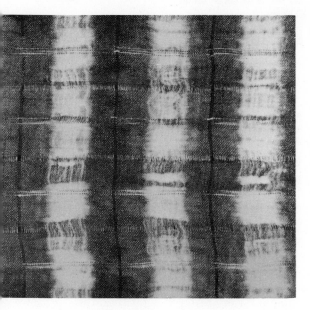

The threads that are drawn out completely before tying up the sample can be dyed a different colour from the main sample. After the sample has been dyed these threads can be used to darn in some of the gaps.

a broken effect to the stripe. Some embroidery threads can be woven in the sample at right angles to the drawn threads. This will give a good contrast of thick and thin areas to your design. When they are finished, trim up the edges of your drawn-thread samples. They look nice with all the edges fringed slightly.

12
DYEING METHODS
FOR TIE-&-DYE

GENERAL REMARKS

Some instructions are given for children
and teachers tie-dyeing under classroom
conditions and will naturally not apply
to those tie-dyeing at home.

Wear an overall or apron and rubber
gloves. If these are not available, a
quickly-made apron from an old raincoat,
pieces of waterproof cloth or any plastic
material can usually be provided. Cut a
piece twice the length of the dress or
trousers. Fold it over at the top. Cut a
hole in it to put over the head. Tie
round the waist. Old, long-sleeved shirts
make ideal overalls.

If rubber gloves are not available, use
wooden washing tongs, old spoons or a
stick for lifting the samples out of the
dye. Place these on newspaper to drain
before rinsing (this cuts down on the
rinsing).

Put newspaper around the whole area
where the dyeing takes place, on the
floor and round the sink too. Rinsed
samples also can be drained, squeezed
and rolled in newspaper, to extract
excess moisture from the samples.

Cover the sample with clean newspaper
when ironing it.

Dye powder kept dry in air-tight jars
should last for a long time. Keep dye
away from the light, in a dark cupboard,
or at least encased in a cardboard box.

Never put wet or damp spoons into a
jar of dry dye powder.

Never put spoons that have been in other
coloured dyes in a jar of dry dye powder
without first washing and drying them.

With most dyes longer dyeing gives
deeper colours. The deeper tones of any
one colour are faster to light than the
paler colours of that dye. Allow for the
sample drying very much paler than it
appears when it is wet.

Where possible, soft water should be
used for dyeing. If the water is very hard
add ¼ teaspoon Calgon to every 1 pint of
dye liquor.

Levelled-off spoon "scoop" measures
are used for the amounts given in the
dye recipes.

Rinsing

The sample needs to be *immersed* in
plenty of water in a bowl or in the sink.
Holding it under a tap of running water
will never rinse it thoroughly.

Chemicals used for dyeing

Common salt   Sodium Chloride

Glauber's Salt Crystals Sodium Sulphate

Calcined Glauber's Salt is twice as strong as the crystals so use half the quantity.

Caustic Soda   Sodium Hydroxide

Sodium Hydrosulphite

Caustic soda and hydrosulphite should be stored in air-tight jars, sealed with Sellotape or Scotch tape.

Common Soda   Sodium Carbonate

These are washing soda crystals.

Soda Ash   The same as common soda crystals but twice as strong.

Use half the quantity stated for crystals.

Useful information

1 litre	1¾ pints and 1000 millilitres
1 oz	28 g approx.
1 lb	453 g

1 litre weighs 1000 g

1 cc water weighs 1 g

1 pint weighs 20 ozs or 567 g

In the amounts stated:

1 teaspoon	5 g approx
1 tablespoon common salt	15 g approx
1 tablespoon common soda crystals	20 g approx
1 tablespoon Glauber's salt crystals	20 g approx

Allow 1 tablespoon of water for 1 oz.

Amount of dye liquor required

In the dye vessel being used decide how far up the side the dye liquor will have to be, to cover the samples being dyed. Put water in the vessel up to that point, then measure it out in pints or litres to find out this amount. When you know the amount of dye liquor required you can estimate the quantities of dye powder and chemicals from the standard recipes. All dyes discussed here can be mixed together, in their *own* range, but *do not* mix household, direct and acid dyes, with reactive dyes (Dylon cold and Procion M dyes).

HOUSEHOLD DYES

Dylon Multipurpose, Dylon Liquid, Drummer, Rit, Tintex dyes, etc. There are others available in different areas. They will dye most fabrics, but check with the manufacturer's instructions when dyeing synthetic fabrics.

Some household dyes are not guaranteed to be absolutely fast to sunlight and heavy washing, but they are very useful for beginners.

The quantity of dye powder given varies. On the leaflet supplied it will state the weight of fabric that can be dyed. The recipes given in this book are based on packets containing enough dye for ½ lb (225 g) cloth (dry weight). This usually means 2-3 yards or metres of medium-weight cloth.

Adjust the quantity of dye powder and water, etc., where packets contain enough dye for *more* than ½ lb cloth (dry weight).

In tie-and-dye, as the cloth is bunched up, only a small area receives the full impact of the dye, the rest is dyed a paler tone. So the dye must be more concentrated or the sample will look wishy-washy. The bundle requires less liquid to cover it than if the cloth were not tied-up. These are the reasons why the recipes given here use less water than those in the leaflet.

Cold and warm dyeing with household dyes

This method is for young children or for any occasion when it might be considered dangerous to use hot or simmering dye liquors. It is also a means of doing tie-and-dye in classrooms where there are no heating facilities and no hot water available.

Cold dyeing with these dyes does not give the full depth of colour that is possible when the dyes are used just below the boil, or very hot, but some attractive pastel colours can be obtained.

Method for Dylon multi-purpose dye

Paste the dye powder from one container (1-2 teaspoons) with a little hot or cold water. Add 1½ pints (1 litre) boiling water and 1 tablespoon salt. Stir until all dye particles are dissolved. See that all the dye on the back of the spoon is dissolved. Make sure that the dye on the bottom of the bowl is also mixed in, because it sometimes stays there in little mounds. Boil up the dye if possible.

Method for Dylon liquid dye

Add 1 pint (½ litre) boiling water to 1 cap measure of dye. Add 1 tablespoon salt.

This dye liquor can now be put into bottles or jars and stored until required. Shake up the contents before using as the dye tends to sink to the bottom.

If the dye can be used *warm* it gives a slightly better colour yield. Suggestions for doing this even without heating facilities in the classroom:

1. Mix up the dye just before the class and cover it with a blanket or similar.

2. Store the hot dye in old thermos flasks.

3. If there is hot water in the school cloakrooms, mix the dye there and bring it while hot into the classroom. Jugs are best for this, to prevent "slopping".

4. If there is a plug for an electric kettle somewhere near, mix the dye in a jug and bring it to the classroom.

5. Stand dye in suitable unbreakable, screw-top containers on the radiator some time before it is needed.

6. If there is hot water, the samples can be "wetted out" in *hot* water before dyeing.

Dye the first experiments for a few minutes. If they are successful extend the dyeing time from 5 minutes up to 20 minutes. Place the sample on newspaper when it comes out of the dye. Rinse. If there is no sink, have bowls or buckets of water ready for the rinsing. Where there is water available rinse the sample in a bowl until the water clears, then drain on newspaper. Dry and untie. For a second colour add to or change the position of the bindings before dyeing.

Hot dyeing with household dyes

Paste dye from one container (1-2 teaspoons) with a little water. Add 1½-2 pints (1 litre) boiling water and 1 tablespoon salt (vinegar for silk or wool as directed). Stir. Wet out the sample if necessary, and dye, just below the boil for 5-20 minutes, moving the sample about at intervals. Place it to drain on newspaper after dyeing. Rinse thoroughly in a bowl until the water clears. Drain on newspaper. Dry.

Change or add to the bindings before dyeing a second colour.

After the final dyeing and rinsing, dry and untie. Rinse the sample again after untying. Put between newspaper to mop up the excess water. Dry partially. Iron the sample with a covering of clean newspaper while it is damp.

When laundering these samples wash in *warm* water plus a little *mild* soap powder or detergent. Mop up excess moisture with rag or newspaper and dry quickly. This will prevent colour from running and staining the white resist patterns.

DIRECT DYES

For cotton, linen, viscose rayon. Some will dye silk and wool. The fastness properties of these dyes vary considerably. The best brands are very fast to sunlight but they may run a little when washed. Warm quick wash only. These are good reliable dyes and easy to use. Each manufacturer has his own brand name for direct dyes. When buying, ask for the colours with a good "light-fastness" rating.

The Solamine range of direct dyes gives good colour yields whether dyed hot or cold (from Skilbeck Bros.).

Hot dyeing

Method: paste ¼-½ teaspoon dye powder with a little cold water. Add 1 pint (½ litre) hot water and 1-2 tablespoons salt. Stir. If this colour is not strong enough increase the amount of dye powder to ½-1 teaspoon. Wet out sample if necessary. Dye just below the boil for 5 minutes for the trial samples. If these are successful, dye for a longer period—up to 1 hour—to get the full strength of colour. Rinse and follow instructions given for household dyes. Direct dyes can be used *over* reactive dyes.

Cold dyeing
(for Solamine dyes)

Method: paste 1 teaspoon dye powder with a little cold water. Add 1 pint (½ litre) boiling water and 2 teaspoons salt. Stir thoroughly. Wet out sample and dye for 10-15 minutes either cold or luke-warm (35°C). Add 2 teaspoons salt and dye for 10-15 minutes. Add a further 2 teaspoons salt and dye for ½-1 hour, or even overnight if possible. The longer the dyeing the deeper will be the colour.

ACID DYES

For silk and wool. The fastness to light varies—some are excellent. Warm quick wash only. Each manufacturer has his own brand name for acid dyes.

Method: paste ½ teaspoon dye with a little hot water. Add 1 pint (½ litre) hot water, 2 tablespoons Glauber's salt and 1 teaspoon acetic acid 30 per cent. Stir well.

Wet out sample if required and dye just below the boil for 10 minutes to 1 hour, or until you have the colour required. Rinse in warm water if possible, and follow the instructions for household dyes.

Most direct dyes and acid dyes *can* be used cold. After mixing, bring them to the boil. Then use exactly as described for cold dyeing with the household dyes. Left-over, mixed household, direct and acid dyes will keep for several weeks in air-tight jars or bottles tightly corked.

USE OF ACETIC ACID

Bought at chemists and drug stores ready mixed up to 25 or 30 per cent strength. Teachers ordering acetic acid for schools may receive bottles labelled "Glacial" acetic acid. Keep this away from children—it is 100 per cent strength. To make 30 per cent strength, add 1 part glacial acetic acid to 2 parts water. Shake to mix. It has a very strong vinegar smell. The 100 per cent glacial acetic acid smell stings your nose—so be careful with it.

USE OF FIXANOL PN

Fixanol PN (ICI product obtainable from Skilbeck Bros.) is used to improve washing fastness. You will find that all dye manufacturers have their own brand of similar fixing agent.

An after-treatment with Fixanol PN or similar produces a marked improvement in the washing fastness of samples dyed with household, liquid, direct and acid dyes. However, the treatment causes a slight fall in the light fastness of the dyes.

Method: rinse the sample after dyeing but *do not untie*. Put enough hot water to cover the samples, in a bowl and add 1 teaspoon Fixanol PN for every 4 pints (2¼ litres). Soak the tied-up samples for 15 minutes at 70°C (160°F), moving them about occasionally. Maintain this temperature throughout the 15 minutes if possible.

Soaking the samples for 15 minutes in a warm or even cold Fixanol PN bath, does improve the washing fastness so that there is less staining of the resists. Remove the samples from the fixing bath. *Do not rinse*—squeeze out surplus moisture and drain on newspaper. The samples can be untied while wet, partially dried and ironed while damp. When the samples need to be laundered, wash in water which is 10° higher than the temperature of the Fixanol bath—do not boil.

After several washes the fabrics may need a second treatment in a fixing bath. This time they will be undone but there should not be too much loss of colour. Alternatively a teaspoon of Fixanol PN could be added to the washing water. Fixanol PN can be used for reactive dyes, before or after untying.

If Fixanol PN is supplied in a metal container, transfer to a screw-topped glass jar—it will keep indefinitely then. Left-over, mixed-up Fixanol which is unstained can be saved for some time to use again.

You can re-dye an opened up sample which has already been treated in Fixanol.

To treat a sample which has been undone, put in a warm Fixanol bath and:

1. If the colours run badly, leave in the warm solution for 15 minutes. Then rinse, and treat in a hotter, fresh Fixanol bath for 15 minutes. Dry without rinsing.

2. If the colours run only slightly, heat up the bath to 70°C (160°F) and leave for 15 minutes. Dry without rinsing.

Samples can be washed at 10° higher than the temperature of the Fixanol bath in which they were treated.

DISCHARGING OR BLEACHING

Household, direct and acid dyes can often be bleached or discharged with:

1. 1 part bleach (household bleach) to 3 parts water or

2. ½-1 teaspoon Dygon to 1 pint (½ litre) boiling water.

Leave the sample in until the colour changes. Do not leave too long or the cloth rots. Rinse the sample thoroughly before and after untying.

A mild bleach solution will usually help to remove dye stains from the hands. A wash in warm water and detergent will also get rid of some of the stains.

REACTIVE DYES

Dylon cold water dyes, Procion M dyes or similar. These dyes give bright colours which are fast to light and to washing on cotton, linen, viscose rayon and slightly paler colours on silk and wool.

Dylon cold and Procion M are similar dyes so can be used and mixed together, making a good range of colours. For these dyes it is essential that the fabric is absorbent, otherwise the dye will not fix properly on the cloth. It is worth washing the fabric to be dyed, in Lissapol D in very hot water for ½ hour. Use ½ teaspoon to 2 pints of water (2 grammes per litre). Soap powder or detergent can also be used. Rinse thoroughly.

Although many teachers prefer the household dyes for cold dyeing with the younger children, there is no reason at all why the Dylon cold or Procion M dyes should not be used from the very start, for tie-dyeing. The short dyeing method (10-20 minutes in strong dye, with or without the polythene bag after-treatment) would give results equal to, or better than, the cold household dyeings. They would also be faster to light and wash better.

After dyeing, the reactive cold water dyes seem to need a great deal of rinsing before the water clears. Soak the samples for some time in a bowl of water. Change this several times before giving them the hot wash. These dyes penetrate rather readily so it is usually necessary to wet out the sample before it is dyed. Bulky samples can be dyed dry.

After untying the sample, occasionally there appears to be no resist. Rinse again and give it a hot wash and usually some pattern emerges.

Dylon cold and Procion M dyes will not dye cloth after they have been mixed for 2-3 hours. In fact the moment that the soda is added to the dyes they *begin* to react. Once they *have* reacted, even if there is no cloth in the dye they will no longer dye the cloth properly. They cannot be resuscitated or made to dye the full colour again.

If these cold water dyes have to be prepared some time before they are used, mix up the salt/soda solution and keep in one container. Mix up the dye with warm water and keep it in a separate air-tight jar or bottle. When you are ready to put your samples in the dye, mix up equal quantities of the two solutions and put the sample in *immediately*.

Dylon cold and Procion M dyes

Standard recipe

In the dyebath dissolve 2-3 tablespoons common salt and 1 tablespoon common soda in 1 pint (½ litre) hot water. Stir. In a separate bowl dissolve 1-1½ tea-spoons Procion M dye *or* 1 small tin (1½-2 teaspoons) Dylon cold dye in 1 pint (½ litre) warm water. Stir until all the dye particles are in solution. When the samples are ready to be dyed and have been wetted out, and *not* before then, mix the dye with the salt/soda solution. Enter the samples immediately.

Method A: long cold dyeing

Dye for 1 hour moving the samples about for the first 15 minutes and then at intervals.

Lift out the samples and let them drain on newspaper. Rinse until the water clears. (A great deal of loose colour comes out at this stage.) Pour boiling water over the sample, add a little detergent and leave for 5 minutes, stirring occasionally. Rinse again thoroughly before undoing the sample.

After untying (which can de done while the sample is wet with these dyes) rinse well. The resists are often improved if the sample is given a second hot wash after it has been undone. Rinse. Finally dry partially, and iron while damp.

Method B

Mix as above. Dye lukewarm. The dye penetrates more when warm or hot but sometimes the colour yield is not so good. Dye and rinse as A.

Silk

Use Method B for silk dyeing at 25°-70°C (77°-160°F). Use 2 tablespoons Glauber's Salt and 2 teaspoons common soda, instead of the amounts of salt and soda given in Method A.

Wool

Dye just below the boil for 1 hour without salt or soda but with 1 teaspoon acetic acid 30 per cent (or 2 tablespoons white vinegar). Another method for wool, using the same recipe is to bring the dye containing the sample almost to the boil, turn off the heat, or remove the saucepan containing the dye from the hotplate and leave the sample in it to cool for at least 1 hour.

Method C: short dyeing

Mix as standard recipe. Dye cold or warm for 10-20 minutes, moving the sample about in the dye. Lift the sample out of the dye, do not rinse, but put it in a polythene bag. Tie up the bag and leave for 12-48 hours at room temperature. Rinse and wash as Method A.

Method D

Exactly as Method C but leave on, or near a warm radiator for 2-3 hours. Rinse and wash as Method A.

Method E

Exactly as Method C. Instead of putting the sample in a polythene bag, wrap it in some newspaper or cloth (do not rinse sample) and bake in an electric oven for 5-10 minutes at 140°C (285°F) or place in front of a fire until bone dry. Rinse and wash as Method A.

The sample can be steamed for 5-10 minutes, if a steamer is available, or even a double saucepan. A small sample can be wrapped in paper or cloth and steamed by putting it in a bowl inside a saucepan of boiling water (with the lid on to keep in the steam).

For the second colour add to and change the bindings and use any of the methods just described. Far more exciting results are possible with these dyes if the sample is untied and completely re-tied before dyeing the next colour. The second or third colour does not blot out the first layer of pattern. So an interesting tracery of overlapping colours is built up.

The reactive dyes do not bleach properly in household bleach.

Suggested Procion M dyes for tie-and-dye

Procion Brilliant
Yellow   M4GS (lemon)

Procion Yellow	MRS (bright golden yellow)
Procion Brilliant Orange	M2RS (flame)
Procion Red Brown	M4RS (deep chestnut)
Procion Brilliant Red	M5BS (crimson)
Procion Brilliant Red	M8BS (magenta)
Procion Scarlet	MGS (scarlet)
Procion Blue	M3GS (green blue)
Procion Brilliant Blue	MRS
Procion Navy Blue	M3RS
Procion Olive Green	M3GS

Colour Mixes

Charcoal black	1 part Brilliant Orange M2RS to 5 parts Blue M3GS
Brown	1 part Blue M3GS to 5 parts Brilliant Orange M2RS
Charcoal	Equal quantities of Dylon cold water dyes A13 and A17

HOW TO DYE PARTS OF A SAMPLE

Some interesting colour schemes are possible if certain parts only of a sample are dyed. There are several ways to tackle this, either before or after dyeing the whole sample. Tie up your fabric and then do one of the following:

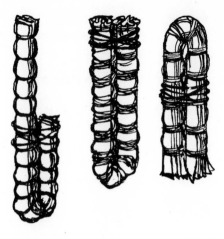

1. Enclose the part of the sample *not* to be dyed inside a polythene bag. Make a firm barrier of binding to stop the dye seeping through. Leave the part to be dyed outside the bag. Tie the polythene bag to the saucepan handle so that the other end of the sample is immersed in the shallow dye.

2. Place a piece of wood across the dye vessel. Tie one end of the sample to the piece of wood or thread it on so that the other end is standing in the dye. In the same way, the sample can be tied to a piece of wire wrapped round the dye bath. For cold dyeing, the wire could be replaced by string tied round the bowl or saucepan.

3. The sample can be tied to some object above the dye bath, so that it is suspended as far as required in the dye. Wire coat hangers are suitable for this.

4. It is possible to dye any section of a long tied-up sample. Make a "U" bend where the colour is planned. Put a binding on to stop the dye seeping upwards. Immerse the "U" bend in the dye. The sample can rest against the side of the dye bath. To prevent it from falling into the dye, use a tall narrow container for the dye, for instance an enamel jug, etc. The ends can also be inserted into the dye.

5. Gather up any knobs or projections, tie them together then invert them into shallow dye.

6. In reverse, the knobs can be left out of the dye and only the background dyed.

7. A sample can be tied at the top to a piece of wood or a wooden spoon which is then placed upright in the dye.

8. To prevent a sample slipping into the dye, attach a piece of string to it. Tie the string tautly to a heavy object just outside the dye bath.

Try dyeing bands of colour on your fabric before tying it up. Use the simple stripe method.

INDIGO DYEING

Indigo dyestuff is insoluble in water. The process of making it into a solution that will dye cloth is called vatting. The dye solution itself is known as the vat.

The indigo is mixed with a certain amount of caustic soda solution and sodium hydrosulphite solution. The hydrosulphite removes the oxygen from the indigo. This is called "indigo white". In this form it will dissolve in the caustic soda solution. This is called the "leuco compound". In this state the indigo has changed from its original deep blue to a yellowish green liquid.

The sample is submerged in the yellow-green liquid for 10 minutes. It is then taken out of the vat and placed in an airy spot, away from the direct sunlight, to "oxidate". The oxygen in the air changes the indigo back to its original form, and it is now fixed as a blue dye on the cloth.

Important points

As hydrosulphite is added to the indigo vat to remove oxygen, every precaution should be taken to keep out oxygen during vatting and dyeing.

1. Use a deep dye vessel with a smallish top rather than a shallow wide one, which exposes too large an area to the oxygen in the air.

2. Use a glass stirring rod or a narrow piece of wood which moves about in the dye gently and without scooping in or causing air bubbles.

3. When not in use, cover the vat with a cloth or blanket and a lid to keep out the air.

4. Lower the samples into the vat very gently, allow them to sink gradually, without splashing.

5. Keep the samples submerged beneath the dye.

6. When adding extra dye, caustic soda or hydrosulphite solution, do not pour it in. Lower the bowl containing it into the vat, sliding the liquid out at an angle.

The dyed indigo cloth is fast to washing but will fade to a certain extent. Several

dips in a medium-strength vat give better results than one dyeing in a strong dye solution. The latter tends to rub off in use.

Always dissolve caustic soda in a little cold water and the hydrosulphite in a little cold or warm water when additives are needed for the dye vat. Do not add the dry flakes or powder to the dye.

The temperature should be maintained at 50°C (120°F) throughout the vatting and dyeing. Do not heat above 60°C (140°F) or the vat will be ruined. Keep the vat in a warm place.

If the vat changes from yellow-green to blue, or there are blue specks, more hydrosulphite is needed. Add a small amount dissolved in water, stir gently and leave for 5 minutes before dyeing. If white specks appear, add a small amount of caustic soda solution, stir gently and leave for 5 minutes. If the vat appears greyish and watery, it is exhausted. This means that all the indigo in it has been used up. Some fresh vatted stock of indigo needs to be added. If the vat has been left for a few days, "sharpen" it with small amounts of caustic soda and hydrosulphite solutions before dyeing.

How to make a small indigo vat

Approx 1 litre or 2 pints

Mix 1-2 teaspoons indigo grains 60 per cent with a little warm water. If indigo powder is being used, mix with methylated spirits, then add a little warm water.

In the dyebath put 1 tablespoonful of cold water. Dissolve ½ teaspoon caustic soda flakes and ½ teaspoon sodium hydrosulphite in this. Add 1¾-2 pints

(1 litre) warm water and stir gently. Add 1½ teaspoons salt to the indigo, then add the indigo to the dyebath without making any air bubbles. Stir gently with a glass rod or stick. Bring to 50°C (120°F). After 10 minutes the vat will be yellow-green and ready for use.

How to make a larger indigo vat

Approx, 6 gallons or 28 litres.

The stock vat

1. Dissolve 4 ozs (112 g) caustic soda flakes by sprinkling them slowly into ½ pint (¼ litre) cold water.

2. Mix ½ lb (225 g) indigo grains 60 per cent into a cream with warm water. Make up to 1 pint (½ litre).

3. Dissolve 3 ozs (85 g) sodium hydrosulphite in ½ pint (¼ litre) warm water.

4. Add the caustic soda solution to the indigo. Stir. Raise the temperature to 50°C (120°F). Gently add the hydrosulphite solution without making any air bubbles. Stir gently.

5. Leave this to "vat" for 10 minutes at 50°C (120°F) giving it an occasional stir.

The dyebath

While the indigo is vatting, put 6 gallons, less 2 pints (27 litres) warm water in the dyebath. A galvanised ware dustbin or similar container is suitable. Add 12 ozs (340 g) common salt and stir. Add ½ oz (14 g) hydrosulphite dissolved in a little water and stir gently.

Lower the contents of the stock vat (now yellow-green) into the dyebath without making any air bubbles and stir.

If the vat is yellow-green and the temperature around 50°C (120°F) dyeing can begin.

Dyeing with an indigo vat

Gently lower the samples so that they are submerged beneath the dye. Leave for 10 minutes with an occasional gentle stir.

Remove the samples and place on newspaper in an airy spot away from the direct sunlight to oxidate for 20 minutes. Dip the samples again for 5 minutes and oxidate for 10 minutes. Repeat the dips until the required depth of blue is obtained. Rinse the dyed fabric in cold water to which is added acetic acid 30 per cent (¼ oz per gallon or 2 cc per litre). Leave for 10 minutes so that the caustic soda is neutralised. Rinse in cold water. Untie. Wash for 5 minutes in hot water plus a little soap powder or detergent. Give a final rinse in cold water.

POTASSIUM PERMANGANATE

These purple crystals which are cheap to buy from a chemist's are useful for early tie-and-dye experiments although they fade easily. They will dye cotton, linen and rayon and are very effective on silk and wool.

Method

Dissolve 1 teaspoon crystals in 1 pint (½ litre) hot water. Wet out and immerse the tied-up samples for 1-5 minutes. Take them out of the liquid and put them on newspaper while they change colour from purple to brown. Several dips build up a deeper colour. Rinse, wash and untie. Rinse again.

Too strong a mixture or too long in the dye tends to rot the fabric.

Discharge method

Dye a piece of flat cloth as above. Dry. Tie it up and bind it firmly. Dip in fresh lemon juice, or the bottled variety, for a few seconds, or until the colour begins to bleach. Rinse well. Untie the sample and rinse again. The lemon juice can be painted on small areas of the tied-up bundle. *Parts* of the tied up bundle can be dipped in the lemon juice.

A very unusual effect is achieved by using a piece of cloth that has already been tie-dyed. It can be a piece that was not very successful as a tie-dyed sample, preferably dyed with Dylon cold or Procion dyes. Dye it flat, as described for the discharge method. It is now brown all over. Dry it and tie it up in some way. Bind it firmly. Put it in the lemon juice. Rinse, untie and rinse again. The tie dye pattern should now show through the brown cloth to form a glowing resist effect.

GROUP DYEING

When several children are dyeing their samples together in the same bowl, it is difficult to make sure that these samples are returned to their rightful owners. Here are a few hints for marking them.

1. Dye samples in groups of six: 1st unmarked; 2nd put one small safety-pin on; 3rd put two small safety-pins on; 4th put one safety-pin on sample and another hanging from it; 5th and 6th pin together, putting one safety-pin on 6th. These six samples can be threaded on a larger safety-pin. Use stainless steel ones.

2. Groups of four samples threaded on a safety-pin: 1st unmarked; 2nd with one small snip on one edge; 3rd with two small snips; 4th with three small snips. Staples can also be used.

3. Groups of six samples. Thread samples on a piece of fine string in a darning needle. Tie string into a knot. Children are told which order from 1-6 their work was threaded on.

4. This could be done on a large safety-pin—the 6th being the last one on.

5. Marks with a ball-point pen sometimes survive dyeing, if it is short, or, cold dyeing.

6. A large number of samples can be threaded on a piece of wire, string, or a circular knitting needle or a stitch-holder as used in knitting. Numbers are given to correspond with the order of threading and the child must remember his or her own number.

7. Attach strings with 0, 1, 2, 3, 4, or 5 knots or loops tied in. Dye these in groups.

8. Strings can be attached to samples. On each string is the child's own item to be recognised—a coloured bead, button, milk top, peg or paper clip, etc.

9. For a short dyeing. Some pegs or clips can be prepared beforehand, each having a string attached. Each child would then be able to clip one on to his or her own sample and hold the piece of string. Have a bucket or bowl of clean water next to the dye bath. Also have some sheets of newspaper against it. The child can take the sample out of the dye, swish it about in the clean water then wrap it in some newspaper until it can be properly rinsed.

When using cold water dyes, dye for 10-20 minutes in strong dye. Each child pulls out his or her sample attached to the string from the dye and puts it, unrinsed in a polythene bag. The bag is

twisted up and a peg put on it. This can
now be left for 1-2 hours by a radiator,
overnight or even for several days in a
cupboard (or in a bowl in case the dye
runs out of the bag). The bag can have on
it the name of the child, or a number.
Finally the sample is rinsed and given a
hot wash.

MIXING SALT/SODA SOLUTION IN BULK

When using cold water dyes, it is bene-
ficial to have a large quantity of salt/soda
solution prepared beforehand to use as
required. This can be kept in a bucket
or large bowl. Stir up each time before
using because a sediment tends to settle
at the bottom.

Mix 1 gallon (4½ litres) hot water with
approximately 1 lb (450 g) salt and
approximately ½ lb (225 g) or 8 tablespoons common soda. When you want
1 pint (approx ½ litre) of dye liquor,
mix 1 teaspoon Dylon cold or ½-1 teaspoon Procion M dye with ½ pint (¼
litre) warm water. When dissolved add
this to ½ pint (¼ litre) of the salt/soda
solution. Start the dyeing immediately.
If the colour is not deep enough, use a
little more dye powder and an extra
tablespoon salt.

13
HOW TO USE
TIE-DYED FABRICS

Large and small pieces of tie-dyed fabrics make all kinds of unusual looking articles.

TOYS

All soft toys, puppets, dolls and any sort of dolls' clothing. Furnishings for the doll's house are the last word in smartness. What about a tie-dyed kite?

CLOTHES

These too are a "must". Shirts, tee-shirts, collars, ties to match, dresses and skirts. Now skirts! What a chance to display all your choice bits of tie-and-dye. Joined together in a patchwork design or appliquéd on a different background, they could be made up into eye-catching garments. You can tie-dye jeans, shorts, cotton socks, beach wear made of towelling, beach bags and handbags. There are so many other ways of using your dyed fabrics—hats, hat-bands, ponchos, belts, collars, cuffs for dresses, hair ribbons, bows for dresses, even dress trimmings, hankies. Scarves of course are taken for granted—long, short, thin, thick, velveteen, wool, silk and cotton sweater scarves, head squares, etc.

In the home, too, tie-dyed fabrics look delightful used for curtains, tablecloths, cushion covers, lampshades, bedspreads, sheets and pillow cases, towels, tea cosies, mats for every occasion, chair covers, book covers, room dividers, bed head-board covers, mobiles, etc.

As costumes for school plays, fancy dress or pageants, tie-and-dye really excels.

CUT-OUT DESIGNS

These are fascinating to do and make interesting panels. Choose some of your small pieces that have a really definite pattern. You need a small pair of sharp scissors and some adhesive. This must not show on the design when it is dry. Make a test on the back of a small piece of fabric. If it shows as a blotch on the front when it is dry, try another kind. The adhesive should be used sparingly. You can try Marvin Medium, Sellobond, Elmers, PVA, or any of the PVA adhesives, Copydex, Multigloy, or ordinary gum. There is a method of sticking down cut-outs and collages but it does slightly alter the crisp look of the white resist. It can only be used on fabrics where the dye will not run or "bleed". So it is alright on fabrics dyed with Dylon cold and Procion M dyes, but not for household or direct dyes. Pin the design on its background. Place this on two or three layers of newspaper.

Dilute two teaspoons Marvin Medium in approximately ¼ pint (140 ml) water. Some fabrics may need a stronger mixture. With a large brush paint this over the whole design, leaving in the pins. If any pieces refuse to "stay put", slip a little stronger Marvin Medium under the edges with a fine paintbrush, press them down and put in another pin.

Leave until almost dry before removing the pins. You may have to stick odd bits down with a little more adhesive. If the pins have left holes in the cloth, wet the area slightly and smooth with the thumb nail. The design can be left on the news-paper backing or be taken off. Trim up the edges.

The designs which are made of pieces of cloth cut with straight edges, can be sewn or machined together.

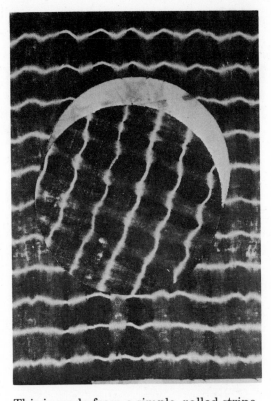

This is made from a simple, rolled-stripe pattern of fine muslin. Iron the cloth on Vilene (Staflex), or stick it on paper. Cut out a circle from the centre. Place the striped cloth on a background of contrasting colour and pattern, which projects about 1 inch all round to make a border. Pick up the circle. Turn it round and lower it slightly so that the background shows through as a crescent "moon". The stripes on the circle now run in a different direction from the rest of the sample. Pin in place then stick the pieces down.

17 *Birds on the lawn* – Background –
clothes-peg or pin method. Birds – cotton
reels for backs and pieces cut from circle
made with small sticks for lower part.
Household dyes used.

18 *Fishes* – Background – any texture. Fishes – clothes-peg or pin method and rubber rings. Household dyes used.

19 *Computer* – Small pieces of fabric dyed in a mixture of methods. Dylon cold water and Procion M dyes used.

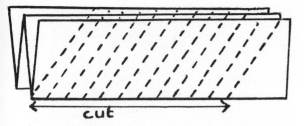

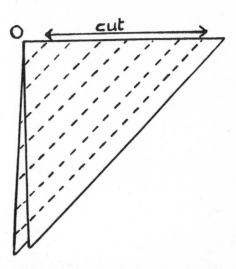

Fold a piece of cloth with a definite tie-dyed pattern into four lengthways. Cut across into diagonal slices. Re-assemble the slices on a contrasting tie-dyed background. Spread the pieces out so that the background shows through. Stick in place.

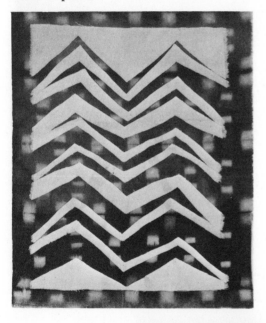

Fold a small square with a bold tie-dyed pattern into quarters diagonally. Cut it into slices parallel with the lower edge. Unfold and place it on a contrasting tie-dyed background. Leave in place the first or outside slice. Lift out the second or next slice and turn it round to form a diamond shape, next to the square. Leave the odd numbers 1, 3, 5 and 7 in place. Pick up the alternate or even numbers 4, 6 and 8 and place them inside the diamond shape. Pin in place. Leave until the adhesive is added and has become dry. Then remove the pins.

Choose a small square or rectangle with a lively tie-dyed design. Fold it into quarters. Cut into curved slices beginning at the centre and working outwards. Place the cut pieces together in order, unfolded on a very bright background. As above leave numbers 1, 3, 5, 7 in place. Remove 2, 4, 6 and place them in order within each other to form a second motif alongside the first. Pin in place until the adhesive is dry. Remove pins.

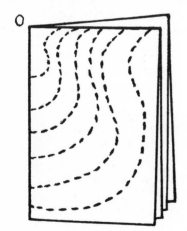

Have ready a tie-dyed background larger than the sample, to be cut. Choose another piece of cloth with a simple bold tie-dyed pattern. Cut a slice from the top of the sample in uneven zig-zags. Pin this on the background. Cut a second zig-zag slice from the sample. Pin this on the background, leaving a small gap in between it and the first slice. Continue in this way until the whole sample is cut up and re-assembled on the background, with gaps between each slice. Pin the pieces down until the adhesive is put on and is dry. Remove pins.

Choose a rectangle of cloth with a simple but very definite tie-dyed stripe design, and a bright-coloured contrasting sample for the background. Pin the background on newspaper, paste on paper or iron on Vilene (Staflex). Make a paper pattern for the cut-out as it must be accurate. A1 must be the same as A2 but the stripes on one should run across and on the other downwards. Similarly B1 and B2 are the same size but with stripes running in opposite directions. On the background place the rest of the striped cloth. Swap the positions of A1 and A2.

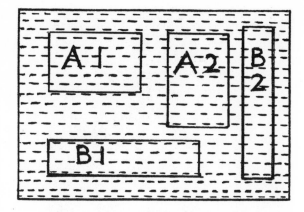

Change over B1 and B2 in the same way. Slide the four cut-out rectangles underneath the striped framework a little way. The background now shows along two edges of each of the rectangles. Pin in place. Leave until the adhesive is dry. Remove pins and trim up the edges of the panel.

The cut-out design above is based on the same principle.

USING UP ODD PIECES OF TIE-AND-DYE

Don't throw away samples that are not too successful, or the odd pieces you used for experiments. There are so many ways of using them. Try the following:

1. Tie them up again using a different method and dye them in a contrasting or darker dye.

2. Or, if the dye bleaches at all, put the whole, or part, of the re-tied up bundles into bleach. Dilute household bleach 1 tablespoonful to 3 tablespoons cold water. Add a little more bleach if it is not strong enough. Remember that bleach rots the cloth if too strong, or if the sample is left in too long. Rinse really thoroughly, before and after untying.

3. If there is a good piece in the sample, cut it out and put it on another background, or use it for embroidery, collage, fabric mosaic, etc. The remainder of the cloth can be used as 1 or 2, or, kept for a background for other work.

4. If the pattern is rather indefinite, emphasise the shapes by painting with pigment dye, or poster colours. If the cloth is not going to be washed, draw on it with a ball-point pen.

5. Use it as a background for other crafts—potato print, linoprint, screen prints, stencil, flour paste resist, batik, machine or hand embroidery. Add buttons, beads and sequins to fit in with the design.

6. Use bits for patchwork. The fabrics can be cut into squares or stripes and combined with good bits of tie-and-dye. Several children can participate in this.

7. Appliqué small circles or spot patterns to form a superimposed design, on a bright, textured tie-dyed background.

8. Make them into toys, mobiles or garments for dolls.

9. Dye in permanganate of potash and bleach (see p. 134).

BONDING FABRICS TOGETHER

There are several products which bond
together two separate pieces of cloth.
These are excellent for cut-outs, fabric
mosaics and fabric collages.

"Ademco" Tissue is a product used by
photographers. When placed between two
layers of cloth and ironed with a hot
iron it bonds the two together. It can be
used to join fabric to thin cardboard. It
is a very fine transparent gelatine-like
substance, sold in sheets.

PANELS AND WALL HANGINGS

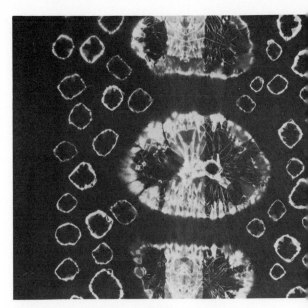

Part of wall hanging made of twill
sheeting. A tuck is made down the centre
of the cloth. Large stones are bound in
the tuck. A border is made on either
side by tying in small stones.

Groups of small stones used as hitches
for the binding-in of large stones. Several
small stones are tied in one corner to
balance the design.

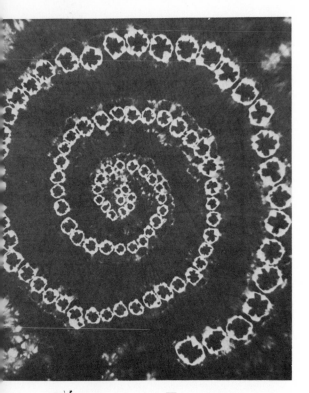

Stones bound into the cloth to form a
spiral design. Very small stones are tied
in the centre. Towards the outside of the
spiral they increase in size. The background is marbled.

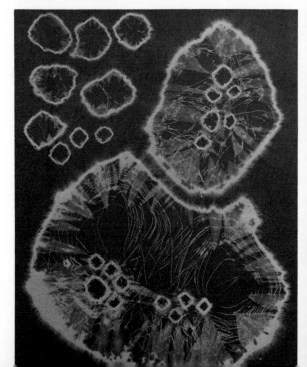

A simple hanging made of twill sheeting, dyed in one colour. The interest relies on the arrangement and differing sizes of the bound circles.

Two tucks are made down the cloth, and two tucks across it. This cloth is placed over a piece of wood or cork and close binding added in all directions.

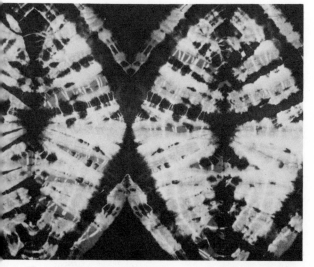

The cloth is folded over double so that the edges meet in the centre. An oval is made on each fold.

This shows an arrangement of four
pleated diamonds made with the safety-
pin method. The background is marbled.

A square decorated with the pin-pivot
method on double cloth.

This shows two lengths of cloth using
easy methods to dye all-over patterns.

Left: Velveteen. Small clumps or
bunches of cloth are picked up and
bound at intervals. Dyed one colour.

Right: The larger circles down the centre
are bound before dyeing the first colour.
The smaller circles are bound before
dyeing the second colour.

Small pieces of tie-and-dye fabrics are
cut out and placed on a background to
make a simple picture. The fabrics are
stuck down with a PVA adhesive. Picture-
making can be a group project.

A picture panel using sewing methods.
The leaves are running-stitch shapes. The
flowers and stems are made with oversewing.

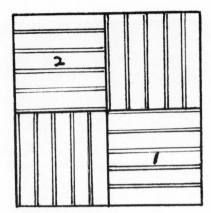

A folded silk square.

These two diagrams show method of making a fabric mosaic. Cut a tie-dyed square in four, then turn two opposite quarters 90° and stick down.

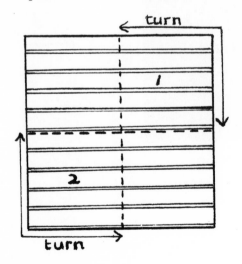

MOUNTING WALL HANGINGS AND PANELS

Wall hangings, pictures, panels, etc., can be mounted in several ways:

1. Make a large hem at the top and bottom, or top only, to hold a dowel rod, or metal rod.

2. Sandwich the edges at the top and bottom for about ½-¾ inch between two narrow strips of wood. Apply the cloth with adhesive to one piece of wood for ½ inch-¾ inch. Then put several small screws along the back to sandwich the cloth between the two pieces of wood and to clamp them together. Make sure the screws do not show on the front face of wood.

3. Stick or sew the hanging on to some coarse cloth—wool, hessian, linen, etc. Fringe this on three sides and put a dowel rod at the top.

4. Stretch the panel or hanging over hardboard, plywood or cardboard.

5. Mount on a stretcher.

6. Put in a picture frame with or without glass.

7. Sandwich between perspex or glass.
There are special fitments for clamping
these together.

8. A small panel will hang on the straight
part of a thin triangular metal coat
hanger.

14

REFERENCE DIAGRAMS

1 Preliminary folding diagrams. Rectangle folded in half lengthways and across (top line). Rectangle folded into three and four lengthways and into quarters (middle line). Square folded into quarters and then into a triangle, and square folded in half diagonally and then into quarters diagonally (bottom line).

2 Pin pivot methods. Single cloth with pin at centre top, at one corner, and at two opposite corners (top line). Double cloth with pin at centre fold, centre cut edges and centre fold (lengthways) (middle line). Cloth folded lengthways with pin off centre on cut edges (bottom line).

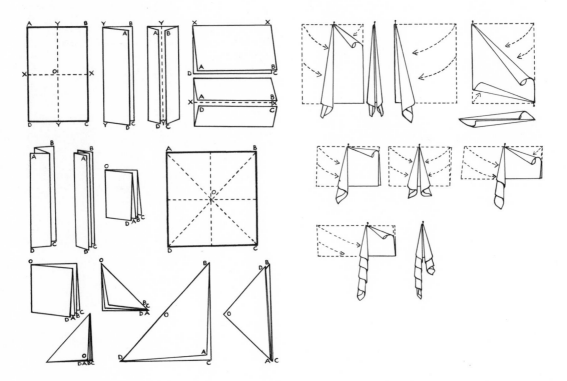

Diagrams showing how to get bands of pattern or stripes in direction of dotted lines.

For bands of patterns use (a) Knotting on rope and (b) Snake method.

For stripes: gather, pleat or roll cloth into a tube and add narrow bindings along it at intervals.

3 Straight rolling on single and double cloth (top line). Diagonal rolling on single cloth and straight rolling with two ropes (middle and bottom lines).

4 Diagonal rolling on cloth folded in half lengthways (top line) in half across (middle line) and in three lengthways, three across and four across (bottom line).

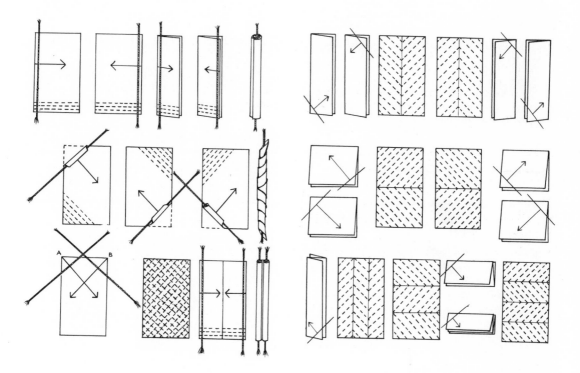

15
WHERE TO SEE TRADITIONAL TIE-&-DYE

GREAT BRITAIN

VICTORIA AND ALBERT MUSEUM, LONDON

Here there are Indian Bandhana samples, Japanese resist-dyed fabrics, the Mary Kirby Collection of African Adire cloths, etc.

THE BRITISH MUSEUM, LONDON

The Sir Charles Beving Collection of West African indigo-dyed samples in the Ethnographical Department.

USA

TEXTILE MUSEUM, WASHINGTON

METROPOLITAN MUSEUM, NEW YORK

SMITHSONIAN INSTITUTE

THE HORNIMAN MUSEUM, LONDON

Has a varied collection of tie-and-dye.

THE COMMONWEALTH INSTITUTE

Has several samples.

All the above have libraries containing books with many historical references to the craft.

16 ADDRESSES OF SUPPLIERS

GREAT BRITAIN

DYES

Dylon International Ltd.,
Worsley Bridge Road,
Lower Sydenham,
London SE26 5HD.

Supply: Dylon multipurpose, liquid dyes
and cold water dyes in small tins, 30 g and
1 lb tins. Procion M in 1 lb tins. Also
chemicals.

Candle Makers Supplies,
4 Beaconsfield Terrace Road,
Off Blythe Road, London, W.14.

Supply: direct and acid dyes in small and
large quantities. Procion M dyes in small
and large quantities. Also chemicals.

Hoechst U.K. Ltd.,
Hoechst House,
50 Salisbury Road,
Hounslow.

Supply: large quantities of most classes
of dyestuffs and chemicals.

Comak Chemicals Ltd.,
Swinton Works,
Moon Street,
London, N.1.

Supply: 4 oz and 1 lb tins of direct dyes,
acid dyes, reactive dyes and others. Also
chemicals and indigo grains.

Skilbeck Bros.,
Bagnall House,
55-57 Glengall Road,
London, S.E.15.

Supply: 1 lb, ½ kilo and 500 g tins of
stock direct dyes, acid dyes, Procion
M dyes (only in kilos), indigo grains and
ancillary chemicals.

Composite orders sent to any country
in the world.

FABRICS

Schools can obtain fabric and thread from
their County Suppliers or Central
Supplies.

Other useful addresses are:

Bradley Textiles Ltd.,
15, Stott Street,
Nelson, Lancashire.

Various cottons, linens, rayons, etc.
(job lots).

Limericks,
89, Hamlet Court Road,
Westcliff-on-Sea, Essex.

Cotton sheeting, towelling, pillow cotton,
calico, etc.

John Lewis Ltd.,
Oxford Street,
London, W.1.

All kinds of fabrics, in household linens
department.

Joshua Hoyle & Sons (Bacup) Ltd.,
12a Golden Square,
London, W.1.

Supply cottons to schools through
county supplies. Many other wholesale
manufacturers will do this.

USA

DYES

Direct and Acid dyes are supplied by:

Dupont de Nemours Co. Inc.,
50 Page Road,
Clifton, New Jersey.

The fixing agent, Cassofix FRN 300, for
Direct and Acid dyes can be obtained
from:

Son Tex Chemical Co. Inc.,
Mt Holly,
North Carolina 28120.

The Reactive dyes Dylon Cold and Procion
M are supplied by:

Farquahar Fabric Dyes,
6 Clarence Square,
Toronto 135, Ontario,
Canada.

ICI Organics Inc.,
55 Canal Street,
Providence,
Rhode Island 02901.

Rit and Tintex household dyes can be
found in most large department stores.